My
UNTOLD TORMENT

My
UNTOLD TORMENT

PIPPA SLOANE

authorHOUSE®

AuthorHouse™
1663 Liberty Drive
Bloomington, IN 47403
www.authorhouse.com
Phone: 1-800-839-8640

Published by AuthorHouse   01/22/2013

ISBN: 978-1-4772-5017-4 (sc)
ISBN: 978-1-4772-5019-8 (hc)
ISBN: 978-1-4772-5018-1 (e)

PROLOGUE

Shrieking with glee, I dashed around the perimeter of the house, trying in vain to escape the icy water gushing from the huge tin watering can my father was brandishing. I giggled in pure delight as he rubbed my bald head, begging my sparse hair to grow. The year was 1966. I was two and a half years old. In retrospect I cannot fathom if these are genuine memories or my subconscious desperately trying to recall long forgotten fantasies I want to believe. Always the pleaser, how can I deny these memories that everyone else seems to hold so dear and visualise so vividly?

I desperately wanted to fit in, and if not for these "memories," I was the only one in my family to have no recollection of my biological father. Both my sisters seemed to have vivid, heart-warming memories of our biological father, who died in a car accident in December 1966. My sisters and mother always waxed lyrical about his kind and generous spirit, saying how he idolised our little family. However, catch my eldest sister, Aleen, ten years my senior, on a bad day and she'd tell of excessive drinking and gambling—either vociferously or in hushed, behind-the-hand, scandalous delight. My mother just turned eighty in 2011 and doesn't have a bad word to utter about her angelic first husband. I am loath to recall the tales, told by her, of my father's excessive drinking and gambling; the loss of his income led to my sisters' just eating bread, resulting in a severe of eczema for my middle sister, Abigail, seven years my senior. She is extremely kind and gentle and never utters a bad word about anyone. On occasion, she'll admit that our home in Warmbaths was often filled with tension and unhappiness.

After my father's passing—an event I have absolutely no recollection of—we moved to Krugersdorp on Johannesburg's West Rand.

My first real memory was of sitting on the pavement outside our house in Krugersdorp, the sky bright blue and clear except for wisps of white, unevenly shaped clouds. I was just four, and as I watched the clouds, I was absolutely sure that my missing father would certainly come down and sit with me on the pavement. Just to chat. I hadn't attended his funeral, and in hindsight, this might have given me some sort of closure or understanding that he was gone for good. An imposing shadow blackened my vivid image. Horrified, I glanced up and saw Mr. McCormack—our lodger—intent on smashing my innocent dream by assuring me that under no circumstances would my father ever visit me!

Mr. McCormack was much more than our lodger. His three sons, Mathew (twenty-three) and Luke (twenty-two)—there were exactly ten months between the two brothers, which, was hugely scandalous at the time,—Mark (eighteen), and daughter Etha (eleven) lived with us. My mother helped look after his children, their mother supposedly unwilling to move to Krugersdorp from Warmbaths. The truth of her abandoning her children was never uttered. She passed at some stage, with none of her children attending her funeral. Sometimes the story was that she passed of mental illness; other times, the cause was given as cancer. Why was the truth never told? I had no idea. My entire childhood was surrounded in secrets, conspiracies, and untold truths.

"Looking after" was relative. My next recollection of that house was of having to sit in the passage while I ate dinner, not being allowed to use the desired All Gold tomato sauce (my favourite, even today). Under no circumstances could I disturb the McCormack's dinner! Thus began years of humiliation, disrespect, discrimination, and lies. The McCormack's absolutely ignored me. No matter what, no matter the circumstance. This treatment caused extreme feelings of inadequacy and inferiority. I was sure I was of no value to anyone. I was wracked with self-doubt, self-loathing, and inadequacy from my preschool years; I knew in my heart of hearts that there wasn't a soul in the world who really cherished or valued my being or even loved me.

As the years passed, milestones began to shape my life. When I was five, Mathew married Joan, and they had a baby two years later. Pipa-Leigh was born the day before my birthday, and she had been named after *me*. This was a great honour in my small, insignificant world. However, this screwed-up notion was proclaimed a travesty of justice by Etha, who often voiced her disharmony. Mathew was the only McCormack, to this day, who was always kind and friendly to me.

Aleen married David in 1973 and went on to have Kate and Shaun. She always was a loner and never paid any attention me, unless she was insulting me or telling me I was stupid and useless; she often used her vicious tongue to publicly humiliate my mother and me.

Abigail married Bruce, who was my absolute hero until my early forties, when he took to treating her abhorrently, slowly alienating himself from me. During my teen years, he was the only constant in my life. He often drove our drum majorette squad around in his car, with his music blaring—he was gorgeous and all the girls swooned over him, giving me the ounce of credibility I so deeply desired. Their children, Jessica and Kevin, were born in 1983 and 1986.

My mother and Mr. McCormack married in 1976, which horrified me. I cried so much; my feelings of despair and frustration grew even deeper.

Even though he had become my stepfather, I was still to refer to him as "Mr. McCormack." What stepdaughter has to call her stepfather by his surname only? To add to my dismay, his children referred to my mother by her first name (Etha told all the local children that my mother was the white maid and I was the "white maid child"). These were defining issues as I grew up, trying to make a small place of peace and harmony in a harsh and very complicated world. I had to polish his shoes daily—a sign of thanks for staying in his house (even after I began working and paid board and lodging). To this day I don't do shoes for anyone at anytime! His controlling manner continued until 1985, when I got married.

From 1969 until 1977, we lived in a huge house in a leafy suburb of Krugersdorp. Besides Mark, Etha, Abigail, and myself, there were often other extended family members crammed into the house. I often had to inhabit a closed off area next to the passage. For the longest time, my maternal granny and I shared a room with Abigail. Granny certainly did not help the very strained, unhappy life that was unfolding around me. She made it quite plain to anyone who would listen that she only liked two of her seventeen grandchildren. She lived with us until 1988, when she passed away, and in all that time, she never once hugged or kissed me. She only spoke to me to admonish me for disturbing her stories on the radio! My most vivid memory of her was listening as she lay in bed at night, smacking her wet lips over her cigarette as she drew deeply on the lethal weapon—the shaft glowing bright red, the swirl of nicotine blackening the wall above her bed.

In 1978, my mother, Mr. McCormack, Etha, and I moved to a double storey house at the top of a hill. I had my own private room for the first time in my life. This was a huge issue, after sharing a room with Etha, who would go ballistic should I accidentally step into "her" space (she also stuffed countless pairs of unwashed underwear into a drawer, which left a distinctly stale and revolting odour in the air morning, noon, and night).

My sanctuary had red and white gingham curtains, and the window looked over gold mines, a sports stadium, and the Hillbrow Tower in the distance. Sitting on my desk, which faced the window, I would imagine another life while drinking in my very own beautiful vista; this was my escape from a very dysfunctional existence.

On a fateful day in January of 1980, new neighbours moved in next door, a Portuguese family. This event would shape my life in a very different way from what I dreamed of as I stared out of my picturesque window.

This family (if one can call it a family) consisted of Lucifer, the father; Aradia, the mother; Roberto, their eldest son (who I would marry five years later); Scorpio, their daughter (who married Marcell four years later, and they had Natasha in 1987 and Cassandra in 1991); Claude, their other son (younger than Roberto by ten years; he married Morrisa in 1996, and they had Polly in 1998 and Tracy in 2002).

I have changed the names of these people at my husband's bidding. I have given them names with meanings: Lucifer, "the devil"; Aradia, "goddess of the witches"; and Scorpio, who can sting you immediately and Claude—lame one, unfortunately Claude lost his back bone when he became involved with Morrissa—the dark one. Not many people will know that this is the story of our lives, and should Roberto's DNA providers (as I call his relatives), and or my "step-family" connect the dots, it will be to their own detriment to acknowledge that this is how they behaved.

This book documents my life with Roberto; my deep-seated feelings of resentment, anger, despair, and humiliation have lessened, and now I have found, much to my great astonishment and persistent annoyance, that I feel sorry for his DNA providers. They have, through their own pride and despicable behaviour, alienated our children, extremely loving, caring, delightful young ladies, and missed out what could have been wonderful family gatherings. By their own behaviour, instead of gaining a daughter and sister, they alienated their son and brother, and they destroyed any relationship with their granddaughters/nieces/cousins: a sad state of affairs by anyone's standards.

There are three phrases I use in this book that I would like to clarify:

"Sharing DNA" does not make one a mother, father, brother, sister, or grandparent—family is defined by treating one another with love, respect, and dignity.

"Experience trumps assumption." We all assume things about people, places, and situations. When one experiences situations and behaviour, one is qualified to document the facts as experience, however unbelievable. Given what Roberto's DNA providers subjected us to, I feel entitled to embellish, thereby ensuring my memoir is not a tale of total hatred and bitterness. If I hadn't found a way, very early on in our relationship, to dig deep within myself and find the ridiculous side to each situation, I surely would have either ended my life or become a total wreck.

"Oizys male." I feel very strongly that a real man treats women, their children, and their fellow human beings with dignity and respect. I therefore refer to males who have no respect for others as Oizys males—the Greek goddess of woe and misery.

Discrimination is widely based on race; there are uncountable stories of white-on-black discrimination. There are also many stories of the black-on-black violence and discrimination suffered throughout Africa, but few examples of such deep-seated discrimination for the pure fact that my husband was born on one continent and I was born on another. We are both white (whatever that means today). His parents escaped to South Africa to make a better life for themselves, although truth be told, they were extremely poor in Portugal, with no hope of ever improving their lot in life.

This is *my* memoir, "biography or historical experience." This memoir is based on my *personal* knowledge, experiences, and feelings. Roberto probably has a different take on these encounters, although he has finally acknowledged that his DNA providers discriminated against, humiliated, and emotionally abused my precious daughters and me in the cruellest possible way.

This is the story of my life of discrimination, humiliation, and utter despair, based purely on fact—embellished somewhat in some places for comic effect. However, every incident is based on actual events. I write without malice. I began writing this book after Oprah advised people to do so as a way to release their bitterness and anger. My frustration with Roberto's DNA providers increased because they have never once acknowledged that they were wrong. Never even a hint of apology for anything. Most of these tales seem unbelievable; however, they are true.

I write this with great respect and love for my two precious daughters—Alexis, who was born in 1988, and Ashley, who was born in 1993. Through no fault of their own, they suffered immense discrimination, humiliation, and hurt. They have always supported and loved me, understanding the complicated, often very unhappy situations we have been forced into.

Roberto has not read a single word of this book. Although he knows that I have written a book about our family, he wants no part of it and will vehemently deny any knowledge of my countless hours spent in front of my PC. May God help him when Aradia starts calling him to complain.

I also write this for my precious mother, who has, in her later years, come to show her loyalty, love, and care for me. She has been more than enough grandparent for my precious girls, giving them her constant love, support, and prayers.

I also write this for Ketiwe, our precious little blessing. Our foster daughter joined our family in December 2007; she often would ask, "Mom, have you written about me being brown and you peach? People will find that interesting." She makes me smile every day! God truly sent her to us.

I want to thank Kate, my eldest niece, who read my first drafts and gave me good sound advice

I want to dedicate this book to every woman who has been humiliated or discriminated against just because evil people think it's their right. Take a deep breath, hold your head up high, and know that you are valued and you are perfect in every way! Take back your power. No one has the right to steal it from you!

On my journey through life I have always walked alongside God. More often than not, there is only one set of footprints, as he carried me for most of my long, hard journey.

OUR FIRST OUTING—APRIL 1980

In January 1980, I was fifteen and in grade eleven, living with my mom, Mr. McCormack, and Etha. As the new neighbours moved in, I watch their comings and goings from the sanctuary of my bedroom. There were copious numbers of trucks and bakkies delivering an assortment of furniture, boxes, and building paraphernalia. There was also a very ferocious dog that drooled, snarled, and barked frantically whenever anyone passed the far gate. God have mercy on us should the dog ever be in the front garden.

I was totally disinterested in this invasion but watched as the male constantly shouted in a foreign language. As time went by, the level of shouting and cursing escalated, directed at his team of workers who re undertaking copious amounts of alterations on the house. The curse of "kaffir" was audible very often. Shocked, I steered clear of any interaction with anyone from the house. However, once in a while I peeped out of my bedroom window into the chaotic back yard. My sanctuary was on the second floor, overlooking their back yard. I loved my sanctuary. It had red gingham curtains, was always immaculately tidy, filled with every memorable nick-knack I held dear. As a young lady, trying desperately to feel valued I kept every special nick-knack to remind me of the good times. Good times were few and far between!

I could hear the father taunting the canine and peered out of my window into their disgustingly dirty back yard. A sneer of evil delight was plastered on his alcohol weathered face. The dog was chained up; he seemed desperate to devour anything or anyone who dared challenge his domain. Sneering with glee at the level of frustration instilled in the said canine, the man disappeared inside and slammed the door. My stomach knotted with foreboding, distrust, and dislike. He was slight of build, with big, gnarled hands. His eyes were beady and shifty. His face was red veined from far too many glasses of hard liquor. His lips were thin and mean.

As time went on, we learned that we must always be wary of this vicious dog. One day, Roberto lost his concentration for an instant and came within striking distance of the still nameless, ferocious canine. Triumphantly, the nameless canine struck, sinking its teeth into Roberto's thigh. Blood spurted out of the four punctures. Lucifer and Aradia found this fiasco immensely funny and praised the canine. This resulted in me driving Roberto to the emergency room even as though I didn't have a licence.

For the longest time, I've known that I have a sixth sense. On several occasions, I tried to discuss it with my mother. She would severely reprimand me, saying, "Sixth senses are totally unbiblical and evil—utter rubbish." Always looking for acceptance from my mother and sisters, I never mention this again—no matter how very strong my feelings were. My sixth sense would inevitably materialise in some form or shape. My premonitions more often than not came true.

One afternoon, I walked into the kitchen, where Abigail was standing at the table, and pronounced, "You're seven weeks pregnant! You'll have a big girl who'll get very sick." As soon as the words were spoken, I literally covered my mouth, wishing I hadn't said anything! Abigail burst into tears and accused me of spoiling her surprise. I was left feeling terribly miserable and confused. Let's face it, where would I have found out that info? True to my pronouncement, she gave birth to a baby girl who came down with meningitis.

There were countless situations, especially in later years with my precious daughters, where I have said, "Be careful of this one" or "Watch out for that one, as he will lie to you, steal from you, betray you." These warnings were based on a strange feeling and the uncanny sense I'd get whenever I met someone. I've never been wrong. These feelings were never wrong, but I would often ignore them, to my own detriment.

The feelings I get whenever I see Lucifer or Aradia are very real. I am consumed with utter fear, despair, and unease. In my innocence I often admonish myself for being judgemental and banish these feelings to my inner core, hoping and praying they'll dissipate.

Soon after the new family moved in, the eldest son introduced himself to me. Sometimes we would chat at my gate. During the April school holidays, Roberto invited me and my friend Sharon to the movies with him and his friend Paulo. We agreed, but oh, to have had 20/20 vision. Why I didn't heed my very deep and intense sense of unease and disquiet?

The movie was a harmless, fun outing. We saw *Kramer versus Kramer,* both Sharon and I shed a few tears and enjoy being offered popcorn, chocolates, and slush puppy. We rarely went to the movies and normally could only share one box of popcorn, so this was a real treat. Paulo paid for everything; he seemed to be very flush.

As time passed, I learned that many Portuguese parents encouraged their sons to "sow their wild oats" with girls who weren't Portuguese, then marry "pure" Portuguese girls. Paulo had an endless cash to sow his wild oats while his chosen Portuguese girlfriend waited patiently at home for him, knowing full well that her intended was out being pleasured by *pades putas* (English whores).

Roberto entertained us with tales about his many hours spent on his beloved citizen band radio. His handle (CB name) was "Venus Fly Trap," and his sister's name was "Sexy Spider!" How very apt. Eventually I became trapped within the very depths of a Venus Fly Trap, the life slowly being sucked out of me, with no possible escape. And Sexy Spider was inviting but deadly! The CB was Roberto's absolute passion, and he had slaved for endless hours working in a clothes shop to be able to afford it. Sharon and I were enthralled, as we had never even heard of this type of communication, and Roberto enthusiastically promised to let us use it one day. However, that day was never to come.

Roberto had promised to give us a lift home after the movie, but instead he and Paulo just gave us bus fare. This was no problem, as Sharon lived near the bus stop and I just needed to walk up the hill. In our innocence, we didn't question why they didn't have to take the bus as well.

3

After an enjoyable, totally innocent outing, I retreated to the warmth and security of my very own sanctuary to read, shutting out the unhappiness that was my home life. I had my own very dysfunctional issues going on in my own house.

Loving fresh air and the early evening sounds as the day slowly winds down I casually opened my window and glanced into Roberto's back yard. Just then, his mother, Aradia, opened the back door. I raised my hand in a friendly greeting and called out, "Hello." I had met her earlier that day at the Mall. To my surprise, she glared at me and shouted, "*Pades puta!*" I did not understanding her comment and smiled back at her, retreating from the window to continue reading.

A while later, I hear the familiar rattling of Lucifer's van returning from a day's work; the vicious snarl of the chained canine was followed by the customary slamming of the back door. Seconds later, I could hear raised voices, including Roberto's. I stop reading and held my breath while straining my ears. There it was again: "*Pades puta!*" interspersed with very guttural, loud shouting in Portuguese.

This was before the age of cell phones, and I was not even allowed to use the house phone, so I had to wait to return to school to ask one of the Portuguese kids what the greeting meant. Perhaps I could learn to pronounce it correctly and shout it out of my window every time I saw them, demonstrating my quick eagerness to learn a new language. There was much slamming of doors inside the house, accompanied by relentless shouting. There was also a rhythmic crash, like something was violently destroyed, which disturbed the stillness of the early evening.

This was in stark contrast to my house, where all conflict or disagreements were handled with a quick dressing down, followed by total silence, with the offending party being totally ignored, sometimes for days (the offending party was usually me). To this day, should there be even a hint of discord between my precious daughters and myself, I insist that we discuss it in detail.

Eventually, silence. Then at regular intervals, Aradia, in her ear-piercing, guttural voice, continued much shouting "*Pades puta.*" Strange how a pleasant greeting can be used so frequently and sound so very offensive.

I spent the next few days in blissful oblivion at Sharon's house. I escaped there as often as I possibly could. In so doing, I avoided the unpleasantness that was my house, at all costs. Being at Sharon's quiet, warm home saved my very fragile sanity and dignity. Stepfamilies can be complicated at the best of times, and mine was extremely dysfunctional. My stepsister Etha never even acknowledged that I existed.
We had lived in the same house for twelve years and shared a room for at least eight of those years. In all that time, we never had a civilised conversation. Etha's only communication with me was through her father, Mr. McCormack. He would then complain to my mother, who in turn would admonish me for my many failings and misdemeanours (unless my transgression was so great that Mr. McCormack would tower above me and demand, in his powerful Scottish brogue, an explanation or apology. I would apologise immediately every time, thereby avoiding more unpleasantness. I was always conscious that my bad behaviour could compromise my mother's happiness. Bad behaviour included not putting the milk in the correct place, or putting the soap on the basin instead of the shower! Oh, that in this day and age, those errors in judgement should be considered a punishable offence; "those were the days, my friends, we thought they'd never end."

My existence revolved around me planning my every move around what suited Etha. Whenever she cooked for herself and her boyfriend, which was every day, I was not allowed in the kitchen. Even if I was ravenous after walking home after a strenuous hockey match, I had to wait for her to be finished. Then I had to be very careful of what I ate or drank, in case I committed the cardinal sin of consuming the tiniest morsel that might be theirs! This extremely demeaning and spiteful behaviour further entrenched my feelings of worthlessness and self-doubt. I was plump in my early teens, and then I became extremely thin in grade eleven. This was the result of being too nervous to venture into the kitchen, never knowing what to expect, avoiding conflict at all costs.

The consequence of this ridiculous behaviour is that now, in my home, anyone can eat anything, at anytime, and we all share all food. There are no rules about how many slices of pizza you may have or how many chocolate biscuits you can consume. Nothing is ever locked away or monitored.

One of the cupboards housed delicious chocolate wagon wheel biscuits. The cupboard was always locked and the key hidden away. These were regularly pilfered by said stepsister, who swore with a dead straight face that she didn't touch the hallowed biscuits. I would then be admonished and chastised for days afterwards for stealing and lying!

After spending a week in Sharon's home, I felt obliged to return to my house. There was an uncomfortable sense of discord emanating from the house next door. Late in the afternoon, I heard a car pull into the driveway next door. Curious, I peeked out of the window. It was a doctor, who entered the house—for once, the door did not slam. This was strange, as few doctors made house calls, especially at night.

Later that night, Roberto was sitting on the dividing wall just off my bedroom window. The weight of the world seemed on his shoulders. After a few pleasantries, he confided that his father had decimated his prized citizen band radio as punishment for taking me, an English whore, to the movies. He then explained that his parents were vehemently opposed to him even speaking to a girl who wasn't Portuguese. Then a few days later, in a fit of drunken rage, Lucifer had sliced Aradia's leg open with a piece of wood. The doctor was there to stitch it up and curb the marching infection. I was totally horrified by this kind of violence. Roberto, however, was totally resigned to it.

To this day, Roberto is unable to stand up to Aradia for anything. He always gives in to her bizarre demands, no matter how devious.

I was really shocked by this turn of events and was sure the doctor would report this to the police. Embarrassed, Roberto confided that domestic violence was common, so there would be no report made.
As the years passed, I learned that this Portuguese "doctor" regularly attended to the wives, daughters, and sons of Portuguese Oizys males who beat them. The payment of a high cash fee always ensured his silence.
In one sad incident, a sixteen-year-old girl had complained of severe stomach pains. This doctor was summoned to the house quite late

that evening. After the examination, the doctor announced that the daughter was actually in labour. The father promptly hauled out his gun, an act I came to find out was very common amongst Portuguese Oizys males. He held the gun to the doctor's head while threatening to blow his brains out for daring to suggest that his daughter wasn't pure. Oh, that being pure was the only wish to have for one's daughter! She soon enough gave birth and was spirited off to Portugal for three months, returning with her "aunt's" baby to look after. So the deceit continued unabated. The young girl eventually married some uninformed young male from Portugal. As customary, during the wedding ceremony, she presented flowers to the statue of the Virgin Mary. This offering symbolised the bride's gratitude towards the Virgin Mary for keeping Catholic girls pure and chaste!

Another bizarre incident happened within a family we knew very well. The eldest daughter was rather large, so no one noticed her expanding girth. One day when I stood next to her, I literally had to leave the room to avoid blurting out, "When is your baby due?" Surely I would have been shot by her father for daring to bring the slightest bit of disrepute onto their wholesome, extremely pure family. One Sunday morning, she announced she was not feeling well and shouldn't be disturbed. A number of hours later, her sister thought she heard strange noises coming from behind the locked bathroom door. They broke down the door and discovered the girl had given birth to a baby boy and was trying to flush the child down the toilet. Shortly thereafter, she was married, the "pure" young bride still presenting Mary with flowers.

After injuring Aradia, Lucifer soon kicked Roberto out of the house for daring to confront him about his violent behaviour. One day, a very sad, confused seven-year-old Claude stood at my gate and confided that he would never marry a *pades*, saying, "It's just too much trouble!" Out of the mouths of babes, never was a truer word spoken.

Not long thereafter, while his family were at the Portuguese club, Roberto asked me to go out with him. Alarm bells clanged as if the hunchback of Notre Dame was having a field day in the bell tower inside my head. I accepted anyway. I couldn't believe that someone actually wanted me as a girlfriend, as my self-esteem was so very low. I told my mother, who only commented, "But you are of different cultures." To me, in my ignorance of the world, different culture meant a different colour. As far as I was concerned, we were both white!

One afternoon, after a strenuous hockey match, I trudged exhausted up the hill; with home in sight, I let my guard down and forgot about the dog. Just then, I was totally scared out of my wits as the insane canine dashed from the back yard, almost bursting through the front gate. I had visions of being torn limb from limb as Lucifer and Aradia gleefully looked on. With God's grace and my speed I find solace behind my front wall. Their evil laughter rang in my ears.

Dogs are said to resemble their owners—too true, the cry resounds.

MY HOSPITAL STAY—JULY 1981

In July 1981, in my final year of school, I had just completed my midyear exams. Relief and excitement engulfed us at the prospect of three weeks of fun, movies, and hanging out at my friends' houses. One day, my dear friend Lucia was spending the afternoon with me, a very rare occurrence as I was loath to bring anyone to my house for fear of some humiliating incident. If my friends discovered what actually went on in my house, I was sure, the humiliation would just be too great. How would I explain to my friends that I was not allowed into the kitchen to eat or drink whenever I was hungry or thirsty? My mouth would go dry, and my face would flush ruby red just at the thought of the utter humiliation.

Much to our surprise, on this day, Mr. McCormack offered to take us to the enigmatic bakery on the main street for an end-of-term treat. Wonders would never cease!

In its hey-day the main street was the longest straight street in the Province with countless teenage boys going to endless lengths to try and get all the 20 or so robots green from one end to the other. Sadly, it is now reduced to a shambles of dirty, falling down buildings and drug peddlers. Motorists are often petrified of stopping at the numerous robots for fear of being hijacked. It was bakery that I had admired from afar for many years.

I recalled with delight, when I was seven, my stepbrother Mathew and his then wife Joan lived above the bakery in a huge, airy, very sunny flat. The love filled lounge over-looked the street. The delicious aromas woke me from my happy dream filled slumber. I never dared ask to buy any delicacies as that would of been rude—especially, after the privilege of sleeping in their new home. What a special treat to have a bed made up especially just for me as nothing was ever done just for me. I relished every moment spent in their cosy; sun filled flat. Not only as the new flat was totally delightful, but because they showed me love and showered me with attention always making me feel valued and worthwhile. Grateful therapy for my broken, insecure soul.

Each time before going up the stairs to their flat I often lingered outside the bakery, peering through the sparkling floor-to-ceiling window, enthralled by the huge area between the window and the counter. The immense floor covered with beige tiles, glass like, always gleamed and exceptionally slippery. There was a ledge along the inside of the window and I dreamed of sitting on that ledge watching the frantic comings and goings of delicious cakes, pastries and bread s while drinking in the delicate aromas. My mouth would water and my tummy would ache with desire as I longingly watched patrons leave laden with blue and white cake boxes. The treats and delectable delights were always for someone else.

So here we are 10 years later. This was the first time I had ever actually crossed the hallowed threshold of this enigmatic empire of culinary desire. Unexpectedly, we were allowed to choose whichever delectable delight we desired. Now this was the greatest treat I'd been afforded in a long time. My pulse raced as my huge eyes darted between all the choices. It took ages to decide on an apple and custard slice. Delicate, cinnamon coated, sweet apple slices were smothered in thick creamy custard, encased in delicate sugar covered pastry. I relished the thought of going home and savouring every last morsel. Just for once, not having to share, a treat beyond all comprehension. For me, it was fascinating and shocking that I could actually have a treat all to myself. If I had known what "orgasmic" meant, I might very well have felt orgasmic!

We got back home and I sat on my bed and slowly savoured this unexpected treat. I felt that for once, I was valued enough to be afforded such a pleasure all to myself. I ignored the tiny voice in my head, which I banished with a firm nod. It warned, "Are you not aware of the slightly bitter flavour of this delicacy?" it whispered incessantly. I would not allow my eternal pleasure to be clouded.

After Lucia went home, I lay on my bed, reading. I began to feel mildly dizzy, sort of groggy; I decided to snooze. Roberto came to visit, and when I stood up, I collapsed. He rushed me to our family doctor. Not sure what was wrong with me, I was admitted to the local clinic under a veil of uncertainty. I was banished to the infectious disease section in the back of the clinic. Never once do I think to mention the prized apple and custard slice. How could such a delight, desired for so long, be anything but perfect?

After two days, I was moved to the general ward. One afternoon, while taking a nap, I sensed someone was looking at me. Very slowly and reluctantly, I opened my heavy eyes. I gasped, stiffened, and tried to focus.
A few centimetres from my face was a huge pair of eyes, attached to a face with the biggest pair of lips and the most humungous afro. This stranger was so close I could feel his breath on my feverish cheek. In drug-induced confusion and horror, I blurted out, "What do you want?"

I then could hear the familiar sound of Portuguese being spoken. I looked to the end of the bed and saw Rosa, Scorpio, and Roberto. The girls were clearly annoyed with me for being rude to their Rosa's dear cousin.

Rosa's parents had immigrated to South Africa in 1964, the same year Lucifer and Aradia came over. The Portuguese families who immigrated to this country kept their circle of friends strictly Portuguese.
Needless to say, I've never seen this person before, and he was really strange looking, but as far as the two girls were concerned, I was rude. Another black mark was carved on my long list of misdemeanours. I was loudly berated for not being friendly and welcoming to this freak of nature, regardless of my weakened state. Too shaken to care, I rolled over and tried to get back to sleep.

In the summer of 1987 Rosa's daughter celebrated a birthday with a swimming party.

While the children were swimming and having great fun, I noticed Scorpio and Rosa making eyes at one another. My senses on high alert

I waited and watched carefully to see who would be their target this time. Fearing for my own possible humiliation and or verbal lambasting I followed their gaze, which rested firmly on the gate where the adored cousin, his wife and their 2 year old had arrived. Hushed communication passed between the two bitches. Their cruel and undermining name calling of the couple being their own secret joke as they utter Tekkie Lips and Fatso, as they are condescendingly referred to.

The two year old promptly fell into the pool. The shaken mom sprang into action and jumped in fully clothed to avoid disaster. Mild panic ensued. Everyone was shaken and very quiet except for the two bitches laughing at the now drowned rat resemblance of the wife of the adored cousin. With an evil glint in her harsh eyes Scorpio suggested loudly that Rosa provide the shaken drowned rat with a change of clothing. Scorpio and Rosa, both being extremely thin relish emphasising everyone's size. Just audibly, to all present Scorpio then said "Oh but nothing of yours will fit over her knees" to much cackling as they ventured indoors. The "fatso" is quite frankly was no more than a size 10.

In 2011 my precious Ashley was 17, grown up and very verbal, she constantly says "karma Mom karma".
Today Scorpios daughter is huge as well as being very unattractive. She complains that she looks just like her father, moustache and sideburns included. As the saying goes, all Portuguese men grow moustaches so they can look like their mothers! Then some daughters grow them to resemble their fathers. Cruel, harsh words, I know, but I've earned my stripes!

As time marched on I have found that good, Portuguese Catholic modus operandi is one of total duplicity. Defend your adored, respected cousin to the death against an innocent mistake. Then as the will takes you be extremely nasty to the person you supposedly adore and respect. Fate accompli. You then attend confession and say 10 Hail Mary's and all ills are forgiven and forgotten.

Fourth day, the hospital nurse suggested I go outside for some fresh air. I was totally delighted and headed out to sit under the trees. I always loved sitting in God's gardens, admiring the surroundings and escaping into a world without unkind, ruthless behaviour. A sense of unease engulfed me, and all my senses went on high alert (remember my sixth sense?). The familiar, unwelcome sound of grinding gears drew my eyes towards the gates of the clinic. Panic gripped me as I watched Aradia drive in. Frozen, I watched her climb silently out of her car, quietly close the door, and creep into the hospital.

Curious, I followed her silently. Shock and fear engulfed my entire, exhausted being. She soundlessly slipped past the nurse's station. Her demeanour was stealthy and devious. She stood motionless at the door to my ward, peeping very carefully around the corner in the direction of my bed. Finding it empty, she ventured into the ward and sat next to my bed, pulling the curtain closed in one swift, silent motion. For the longest time, there was complete silence and stillness. Rooted to the spot at the door, I watched, awestruck and confused. Her hand appeared from behind the curtain and grabbed my file, pulling it back into her hiding place. The ugly, offending hand then reappeared and replaced the file.

I could hardly breathe. Totally shocked, frozen in time and space, I watched as she crept out from behind the curtain and silently sidled past me. As usual, she totally ignored me. Her demeanour was now triumphant.
Later the doctor was surprised to find that the page with my blood results had disappeared. I was too embarrassed to explain.

The nurse asked, "Who is the woman who comes and stands at your door every day while you sleep? She just stands and stares at you. She never greets anyone or responds when we ask what she wants."
Mortified, I assured them I had no idea who it was.

That day, test results confirmed that I had had severe food poisoning. Those delectable aromas, scrumptious flavours, and delightful visions from the bakery; once again, I realised that there was an evil, deceitful underbelly to everything in life.

All that glistened was not gold.

ROBERTO'S PORTUGAL VISIT—SEPTEMBER 1981

By September 1981, Roberto and I had been an item for more than a year. It had been a confusing thirteen months for me, as all I ever wished for was that his family would treat me like part of their family. I really thought that when I started going steady with someone, I would automatically gain a real family, especially the father figure I so desperately coveted. I couldn't understand why Roberto's DNA providers were so vehemently opposed to me. I thought that their attitude would change as they got to know me. I secretly considered becoming Catholic, thereby gaining their approval. How truly dumb I was!

In September, Roberto was whisked off to Portugal for a "family holiday". When they arrived at the house of his aunt, Aradia's sister, he noticed some photos of him and I, which had disappeared. His aunt was very vague about the photos and changed the subject. On the second evening of their visit, the entire family was invited to some obscure person's house.

Aradia took Roberto into an old house; after they entered, she ducked out and locked the door. Roberto was locked inside, in total darkness. The windows were all boarded up and a pungent smell permeated every corner of the room. He was totally confused and very scared. He frantically bashed on the door, trying to break it down while shouting to be released. His desperate pleas fell on deaf ears. Silence. Then the evil, demented voice of a *brouche* (witch) shattered the silence. Roberto later found out that the brouche had been solicited by his DNA providers to ensure that he forgot about me totally.

The room was filled with smoke; the *brouche* circled the room with a foul-smelling potion, while chanting evil curses and commands, meant to rid me from their lives forever. Why? Because I was South African—English—not Portuguese.

Portuguese are generally extremely superstitious, despite professing to be devout Catholics. Each generation passed many superstitions to the next generation. They often cast evil curses on people and visit broaches for assistance.

There are countless tales of how superstitions have manifested themselves in their lives. I met a young Portuguese woman when I moved to Standerton, who had been forced to marry her much older first cousin. She had been sweeping the floor and hit her foot with the broom by mistake. The superstition goes: if you sweep your feet you'll never get married unless your mother shouts out a man's name; if a man with that name comes through the door shortly thereafter, you must marry him. Her mother had shouted out a name, and her much older cousin, having the same name, walked through the door. They were married two weeks later.

For most Portuguese parents, it is a fate worse than death for their son to marry out of their "pure" culture. However, should one ever discuss the very mixed origins of the Portuguese, they become apoplectic! It is well documented that the Portuguese are descendants of various nationalities. Until the turn of this century, Portuguese daughters rarely married out of the pure culture, as they were ruled with an iron fist. All Portuguese girls were supposedly absolutely pure when they get married, never even having held hands with their future spouse! Should a Portuguese girl conceive before wedlock, great lengths are gone to, to ensure that no one knew about it.

Three anecdotes spring to mind:

In August 1980, the year Roberto and I started dating, he turned eighteen and there was a birthday party at his house. Aradia caught Scorpio standing too close to Marcel. Ignoring the house filled with guests, Aradia physically dragged Scorpio through the lounge, screaming abuse in Portuguese. The entire spectacle was totally ignored by her Portuguese friends. I was horrified and started to spring to her rescue, but Roberto stopped me. Aradia then proceeded to beat her with a shoe while Rosa and a few other girls looked on, unfazed and totally accepting. Apparently, Scorpio had broken the rule: no matter what, no physical contact until after the marriage ceremony! (Of course, Roberto was born a mere three months after his parents were married.)

In 1989, we attended the wedding of Jose and Maria; their families had been friends since immigrating to South Africa in 1964. The couple had lived together for two years before getting married. I mentioned to Roberto's DNA providers that it seemed blasphemous for her to present the Virgin Mary with flowers, as they had been sharing a bed.
Aradia went ballistic, bellowing, "No, she Portuguese—she pure when marry!"
"But they were living together," I said, daring to challenge her.
"No, she Portuguese, she pure," Aradia responded. "Portuguese girl no do fore marry, only you pades putas." She sniffed, grunted, and shook her head vigorously to rid herself of such evil suggestions.

Rewind to 1977, in my grade eight maths class; this pure bride sat behind me and took great delight in regaling me with the juicy details of her regular trysts with a local biker named Steve. I was totally innocent and shocked to the core that girls did those things. Pure? I'm not quite sure! That is where I learned in great detail how fellatio is performed—to my great horror and shame. Relishing my shock and disgust, Maria took great pains in telling me tales of her experiences with lesbians and three-in-a-bed sex. We were living in the 1970s, and lesbians were virtually unheard of in our sheltered lives. Sex was never mentioned in my house. Sharon and I often secretly discussed this newfound information, wondering if one day our husbands would expect the same of us and certain that our parents never participated in such depraved behaviour (neither of us dared to ask our parents if it was actually true).

In December of 1993 our middle daughter Ashley was born. During August of that year, Aradia announced that Roberto's cousin from Lisbon, Otilia married. Otilia is a sore subject for me as after the Portugal holiday everyone made it quite clear that they would all of preferred

Roberto to have married her. Every photo featured Otilia hanging all over Roberto or sitting on his lap with her arms draped around his neck—him looking decidedly uncomfortable, Scorpio making sure she showed me the photos a million times. The fact that Otilia and Roberto are first cousins no factor. The only factor being that she is Portuguese. At that stage it was quite common for Portuguese cousins to marry. The only criteria were that they were both Portuguese.

A few days before Ashley's birth his mother was delighted to announce that Otilia had had a baby. I can't resist—"Oh so she WAS pregnant when she got married", my angry, frustrated inner being was delighted to point out the obvious. 'No (sniff), no she no pregnant fore marry (grunt), Portuguese girls no do that (snort) all Portuguese girl she pure" I just couldn't let this go! Futile I knew, but longing for some small hint of acknowledgment that Portuguese girls are also just human, and that having sex before you get married is not the end of the world as we know it. "But she only got married in August" I query rhetorically. "No! No! you lie Portuguese girls no do fore marry—*Mio Dios*" (My God) . . . . sniff, snort, vigorous shaking of the head."

Oh well obviously Otilia was blessed with a miracle very premature baby that didn't need any medical assistance." I retorted sarcastically. Note to self—not only are Portuguese families inordinately cruel and conniving their babies are extremely resilient and can withstand anything. Lord have mercy, God have mercy!

Eventually the *brouche* finished her spell and Roberto was released from the room, and his mother handed him a slip of paper—with the name and phone number of the best hooker in the area, who would keep him entertained for the duration of his holiday.

Roberto tore up the paper and threw it in the fire; Aradia, who professed to be the most devout, holy Catholic ever to have graced the earth, physically attacked him, berating him for ruining their family's reputation and status within the community. Then she proceeded to dissolve into uncontrollable sobs.

In hind-sight, if his family had just left us alone, our relationship would have fizzled out. Roberto and I are extremely different, we never should

17

have married. Their constant ranting about me not being Portuguese made Roberto defy their authority and stay with me. So their crude, evil doings actually pushed us together.

Most people know about the discrimination between whites and blacks. However, the subtle, soul-destroying discrimination of one culture towards another is far more powerful. This relentless, intense emotional abuse was unseen to the naked eye, but for the person being abused, it cut deep into my being, destroying my spirit and soul. The scars never healed.

I was totally oblivious to the number of times that his mother's demonic conjuring were to haunt me, cause untold distress, and wreak havoc on our lives. Should I have had the slightest inkling of how very powerful and destructive this evil would be, I surely would have run for the hills and married a nice, unassuming African man!

OUR WEDDING—MAY 1985

Roberto and I were married on Saturday, 25 May 1985, just over five years after our first outing. Roberto had asked me to go out with him officially on the 17 August 1980, and on 17 August 1983, we had become engaged.

The sadness and confusion that I felt on the evening of my engagement is forever etched into my soul. For all intents and purposes, I should have called off our relationship that very night!

Roberto took me to a fancy restaurant and presented me with a beautiful ring. If nothing else, my ring is exquisite! I still receive compliments for it.

After our dinner and the excitement of now being engaged, we went to visit Roberto's DNA providers. On entering their house, I excitedly ran into the lounge with my left hand outstretched, showing off my sparkling addition, enchanted with my new status.

I ran up to Aradia, grinning like a Cheshire cat, expecting her to get up and embrace me; instead she folded her arms over her ample bosom and pointedly looked straight past me, continuing to watch television. I was invisible while she totally dismissed me. Feeling like I had been kicked in the solar plexus, I turned to Lucifer, expecting a warm embrace from him. Instead he started ranting and raving at Roberto in Portuguese, turned on his heel, stormed off, and proceeded to slam the bedroom door with a force that made the house shake to the foundations.

Scorpio then barged into the lounge; her potty mouth twisted in hatred, she sneered, "What the fuck have you done now? You fucking idiot!"

Ten-year-old Claude looked up from where he was playing on the floor and said quietly, "You see? I told you I'd never marry a pades."

Roberto's face was ashen, his eyes minuscule; he was shaking. For the first and the last time in our entire relationship, he stood up for me, putting his arm around me and leading me out of the house, ignoring his DNA providers.

Shaken and scared, we then proceeded to my aunt's flat, where she and her boyfriend popped a warm bottle of cheap Champagne while singing congratulations and celebrations, totally off key but with great gusto. I was so very naïve; I thought that with time, Roberto's DNA providers would come to love me, once they knew the kind, loving, trusting, generous soul that I was. Why didn't I listen to the quiet voice whispering in my ear? You cannot stop a horse once it has bolted. A leopard never changes its spots.

The date for our wedding was decided for us by my cousin Janine, who was also to be my bridesmaid. In October of 1984, she came to visit me at the travel agency where I worked. Looking at the calendar, she said very plainly, "May is a good month to get married in. It still gives Abigail time to make the dresses. Let's do it on the 25th. That's after your period." And so the date for our wedding was set.

Roberto's DNA providers made it very clear from the onset that they weren't going to pay anything towards the wedding costs. However, after Roberto begged and pleaded, they agreed to a very limited budget for drinks. I wanted a small, intimate affair with close family and just a few good friends. As time marched on, the guest list exploded. Roberto's DNA providers insisting that all their associates be invited, constantly adding guests, their reasoning being that if this one was invited, then that one had to be invited.

Many years later I was watching a local Wedding Show on television, which show cased spectacular weddings of ordinary people. This episode showed a Portuguese couple's spectacular wedding—750 guests, a wedding dress that cost tens of thousands of Rands, a venue that was spectacularly draped and hung with swarovski crystals and delicate, breath taking orchards adorning the lavish tables.

While interviewing the Grooms parents before the wedding the presenter asked "If your son was marrying an English girl would the wedding still be so lavish?" The parents almost chocked and stated unequivocally "Absolutely not. If he shamed us by marrying a South African girl we certainly would not have a wedding like this!"

It fascinates me that thousands of Portuguese national immigrated here in the 50's, 60's and 70's to make a better life for themselves and their children. However they mostly refuse to take on South African citizenship, many of those immigrants can barely speak English and they are loath to accept their off spring marrying a South African!
Roberto also became unreasonable, insisting on inviting all the riffraff that were his "friends." These reprobates abused English girls, wooing them with promises of eternal love and devotion, only to dump them as soon as they had gotten enough sex out of them (often giving these unsuspecting young girls sexually transmitted diseases). Portuguese fathers openly encouraged their sons to sow their wild oats with the *pades* girls but only marry a Portuguese virgin!

These friends of Roberto's couldn't stand me. Firstly I openly challenged their use and abuse of the *pades* girls; I also vocally challenged their violent, drunken behaviour. They, in turn, referred to me as the virgin ice queen, as Roberto and I were not sexually active, I didn't drink or smoke, and I vehemently disapproved of their constant drug use. When they realised that Roberto was actually serious about a *pades* girl, they then just totally shut me out and were openly rude to me.

Years later, I met up with Juan, who had married (and then divorced) Rosa. He was different from the riffraff, being ten years older than us. He was really friendly to me, which surprised me. He noticed my confusion and explained that everyone had told him to ignore me, as I was a total bitch; if he did dare speak to me, Rosa would ignore him for days on end! He confided that Rosa had told him that Scorpio had pressurised Rosa into being nasty to me! What a bunch of spineless cowards.

Planning the wedding was extremely stressful. Roberto was totally uncooperative, and it was impossible to discuss anything with him. He had a way of totally ignoring me when I tried to discuss anything he didn't agree with. His favourite line was, "There's fuck all to discuss." That would end the discussion. He would then ignore me for hours on end. I was so very insecure that I never challenged this degrading, despicable behaviour.

For years I had witnessed this type of behaviour from Mr. McCormack, who would argue relentlessly with my mother and then ignore everyone for days on end; my mother would remain stressed until he would deign to speak again. Etha also ignored me. I was totally invisible to her, except for when I did something to make her angry. She would run to her father, and then I would bear the brunt of his anger.

I had no one to discuss this with and just quietly went along, pretending to the world that all was well within the emotionally destructive, very lonely realm I inhabited.

I tried several times to discuss this situation with my mother. Sadly, she just brushed this behaviour under the carpet, insisting that Roberto would calm down once the stress of the wedding was over.
In an attempt to gain favour from Roberto's DNA providers, I decided to convert to Catholicism. Needless to say, this was totally futile; it made no change in their attitude and behaviour towards me at all. In hindsight, the process was a total waste of time! Once a week I dutifully went to conversion classes with the local priest. He would read pages and pages of the history of Catholicism to me while I tried in vain to take notes. I occasionally broached the issues I was having with Roberto and his DNA providers, and the priest swiftly brushed my concerns under the carpet, saying, "It will improve after the wedding. Roberto will change once you're married."

Today, with all the inspirational talk shows, informative magazines, and self-help books, we all know that "your man" will not change once you are married. If anything, the emotional and spiritual abuse will only get worse.

Eventually the guest list was finalized: 250 people, most of whom I did not know. The only good thing to come out of this spectacle was that all my maternal cousins, aunts, and uncles were included. Mr. McCormack insisted on paying for the retinue's dresses, and I ended up with Janine as my bridesmaid, Sasha—a long-time family friend—as my flower girl, and my nieces Kate and Jessica, together with Sarah and Jane (Luke and Mark's daughters), as little attendants. Roberto had Pedro and Claude as his best men. What a joke! Claude proceeded to openly sulk throughout the entire event. The photos are living proof of either his conspicuous absence from the photos or his scowl peering into the lens. Shaun was the ring bearer.

The venue was decided on and the menu chosen. Aradia and Lucifer were disgusted, as it was a buffet-style meal. Their esteemed Portuguese friends had never been to a function where they would have to serve themselves. What a travesty of justice. What an insult to these sophisticated socialites. Most of these people barely spoke English, and their only outings were to the local Portuguese clubs. Roberto, Lucifer, and Aradia seemed to have forgotten that it was my mother paying for this entire shindig.

The Wednesday night before the big day, Pedro had planned the bachelor's party. I was really nervous about this, as I was sure they would turn it into something absolutely disgusting. No one who was at all close to me was invited, ensuring that I had absolutely no idea of what would go on. I enlisted the help of my good friend Stella, whose husband Paulo found out that Pedro had arranged for two prostitutes. The devious, degrading plan was for the prostitutes to have sex with Roberto in front of all the Portuguese reprobates! Scorpio and Marcell knew all about these plans and wholeheartedly went along with them. By the grace of God, Paulo interceded and brought Roberto home before anything took place. Pedro was furious, as he still had to pay the prostitutes! His unbridled contempt for me deepened.

Abigail had made all the dresses. Mine was a beautiful hand-beaded fitted dress with a five-metre train and veil. It was delicate and stylish, absolutely breathtaking. The attendants' dresses were similar to those worn by Princess Diana's attendants, in blue and purple taffeta.

The flowers were done by Aleen. This was a huge compliment for me, as Aleen rarely acknowledged my existence. The little girls carried woven baskets filled with tiny rose buds and carnations surrounded with moss. They were pretty and soft, just like the troop of little girls. Aleen also made button holes and corsages for Roberto's party.

As I walked into the church, accompanied by Bruce, who gave me away, I noticed that none of Roberto's party were wearing the button holes or corsages. Instantly I was engulfed in a sense of fear, as I was sure Roberto would be furious at their absence. Never fear! Whenever Aradia, Lucifer, and Scorpio were involved, there was sure to be a cruel, nasty explanation. On the way to the park for photos, Roberto casually told me that the button holes and corsages weren't properly made, so Aradia had thrown them all away!
We spent hours in the park taking photos. Roberto and I had agreed beforehand that the photo session would only be an hour; true to form, he did as he was instructed by his DNA providers, and we spent three and a half hours taking hundreds of repeat photos. I was too scared to voice my discord in case Roberto decided to ignore me for the rest of our wedding day.

The videographer had given us a choice of having the video done in Betamax or VHF format. After chatting to Bruce he suggested that we go with VHF as he had heard that Beta would be phased out soon. Roberto and I discussed this at length and jointly decided on VHF format. In July when we picked up our video I was shocked to notice it was Betamax. I immediately told the videographer that he would have to make a plan and transfer it to VHS as that is what we had requested.

Roberto was deathly silent. His eyes were miniscule and the furrow between his eyes deep. I knew instantly that the video had been recorded on Betamax on Roberto's instructions. Marcell had told Roberto that Betamax was the better format so Roberto had changed the arrangement that we had made together. Sadly, today I can-not get my Betamax video transferred to DVD. Everyone who has that skill only transfers from VHS to DVD. True to form there was "fuck all to discuss"!

Exhausted by the extended photo session, we arrived at the hall. Roberto made me wait outside, but I was concerned, as the guests had already waited so long. I also noted that Lucifer and Aradia, along with a group of their close friends, were scurrying in and out of the hall.

On entering the hall, I learned why; much to my mother's disgust, Aradia and Lucifer had placed mountains of Portuguese delicacies on the tables where their friends sat, pointedly leaving out all the other tables. The blatant rudeness defied comprehension. On the main table, there were three bowls strategically placed: one in front of Roberto, one in front of Aradia, and one in front of Lucifer!

The rest of the evening, Aradia kept sneaking in bottles of alcohol, which were hidden in her huge handbag. They had bought the bottles from a friend's liquor store, as they refused to pay the venue for the drinks! They didn't see any problem with being so openly deceitful and spiteful. This was truly a show of devout Catholicism. True Christian behaviour beyond compare.

With God's grace, the dinner went off smoothly, with minimal complaining from the DNA providers. Every now and again, they voiced their indignation at having to serve their own food. To keep them happy, the groom ran up and down, serving for them. Scorpio looking on with glee, like the cat who ate the cream.

When the dancing started, Roberto and I had the first dance, which Aradia cut short after a few seconds to dance with Lucifer. She also danced with Roberto for a very extended period, forcing me to dance with Lucifer. To my surprise, he was quite nice, saying that he was happy to have me as a daughter, that he would always support me, and that if there were any problems I should just go to him. When I mentioned this chat to Roberto, he just gave me a quizzical look and remained silent.

I was in seventh heaven, stupidly thinking that he was being genuine. I thought perhaps the priest and my mother had been correct, everything was going to be just fine. Even still, a quiet voice was repeating in my head, "A leopard doesn't change its spots."

Actually, only three months into our marriage, Lucifer totally denied ever having had that conversation with me (I had gone to him in tears after Aradia and Scorpio had been being really nasty to me for no rhyme or reason). I was totally gutted. Roberto just gave me a look as if to say, "I told you so."

Throughout our married life, Roberto often totally ignored me to focus on his DNA providers. Here are a few examples:

In 1999 Alexis (aged eleven), our eldest daughter, was invited to visit a friend in Italy. With great excitement, Roberto, Ashley (five), my mother, and myself accompanied Alexis to the airport to see her off. We were all excited, and Ashley was really looking forward to seeing the plane her beloved sister would take off in. Besides all the excitement, I was quite emotional at the thought of my precious gift from God going off all by herself. She had a stopover and had to change planes in Paris. The flight was a total of sixteen hours.

Alexis had already gone through customs when all of a sudden, Aradia and Lucifer appeared at Roberto's side. My heart sank, but we continued upstairs to go and see the plane off. I was a bit weepy and just needed Roberto to put his arm around me and reassure me that Alexis would be fine. Instead, every time I tried to get his attention, Aradia or Lucifer would speak to him, and he eventually moved over to stand with them. So Ashley didn't get to see her sister's plane take off, as I was too short to hold her up high enough to see over the barrier. I didn't have a reassuring, supportive arm around my shoulder as my precious daughter left. True to form, I was left to deal with the situation and my emotions all alone.

As another example, in August of 1995, Mr. McCormack passed away. Over the years, especially since Alexis's birth, we had become extremely close, and when Ashley was born, she stole his heart. This turn of events healed past hurts, and when he passed, it was an extremely sad time for me. As I got dressed for his funeral, I was exhausted, both physically and mentally.

The funeral was huge, with hundreds of people attending, besides all the bizarre dynamics that made up his "blended" family—his children and my mother's children. I had nursed Papa, as we now fondly referred to him, through the ravages of cancer that reduced him to a bag of bones I could lift by myself.

After the funeral service, I needed to just reflect and relax. I eventually found Roberto, speaking to his DNA providers. I waited for a break in their conversation and then asked Roberto to have a cup of tea with my mom and me. He totally ignored me and carried on speaking to his DNA providers as though I wasn't even there. Shocked, I thought that he hadn't heard me and so I repeated the request, which was greeted with his telltale glare I had become so very accustomed to. I knew full well that I should just leave or face Roberto's wrath later, so I scurried off to support my mother by myself.

From the age of turning 50 many people like to mark reaching each decade with a party. The parties becoming more meaningful as the decades tick by. When my precious mother turned seventy in 2001 my sisters and I planned a delightful luncheon inviting her close friends and all her siblings. Always one to do the correct thing my mother insisted that we invite Roberto's DNA providers. However quite frankly I was far too scared to verbalise that I really didn't want them present!

The afternoon was sublime. My mother was in her element. All of my aunts and uncles have always really liked Roberto and have always showered him with love and attention. Half way through the afternoon Roberto disappeared and my aunts kept asking where he was as they wanted to chat to him. After wondering around the venue I found Roberto outside with his DNA providers discussing a half built pool. I asked Roberto very nicely to come inside as everyone was asking for him. He ignored me. On repeating the request I was greeted by his tell tale glare. I turned and went back inside telling my extended family that Roberto had a terrible head ache and was getting some fresh air. I was loathe to suffer another one of his mood swings.

By 2011 when my precious mother turned 80 I absolutely refused to have Aradia, Lucifer had since passed, at the celebration. Roberto had the time of his life with my aunts, my uncles having all passed, and we still have a stupendous time looking at the photos of him fooling around on the dance floor with all and sundry! I was delighted that the day passed without a single tell tale visual dressing down!

Back to the wedding:

The first dance over, the floor was opened to all the guests. Scorpio positioned herself near to Roberto constantly ensuring that another

Portuguese woman, young or old kept Roberto on the dance floor, effectively keeping him from dancing with his new bride.

My eldest cousin's husband noticed this and came to my rescue dancing with me and all my cousins joined in. We were having a whale of a time when a Portuguese reprobate that I had never even seen before came and started dancing with me. In good fun I accepted his invitation to dance. In a flash he was trying to open mouth kiss me. I was shocked and horrified trying to push him away but he was very strong. By the grace of God my cousin's husband, a giant of a man, stepped forward, grabbed him by the scruff of his neck, displacing him from his position of power. Out of the corner of my eye I saw Jose and his entourage laughing. Sadly my cousin's car was keyed with a despicable profanity. Roberto refused to ever enter any discussion about my ordeal claiming I was exaggerating.

Eventually, it was time for the speeches. Nothing was done traditionally, the way I had wanted. Roberto made a speech in which he thanked his DNA providers for everything they had done and only briefly thanked my mother. According to his later excuse, "in the stressfulness of the moment," he "forgot" to say anything endearing about me! I dearly wanted to acknowledge my biological father. This too was forgotten. The speeches were a cacophony of the riffraff singing incredibly rude songs filled with foul language. To this end, I am sure Roberto is pleased our video cannot be transferred to DVD, otherwise he would be forced to explain to his daughters his never acknowledging me and the riffraff's despicable behaviour.

In hindsight, the most prominent memory I had of my wedding day came before everything happened; it was as I was sitting at the hair dresser at seven o'clock in the morning. There was absolute silence. There was absolute stillness. The only sound was a small, persistent voice repeating, "This is surely the wrong thing to go through with. Call off the wedding now." I just didn't have the gumption to call it off. I knew then that the emotional and spiritual abuse would only intensify. I had absolutely no one to confide in.

As I stood at the threshold of the church, I knew, with every fibre of my being, that I was making the biggest mistake of my life. It turned out to be a mistake that caused me incredible heartache and broke my fun-loving, trusting, easygoing spirit. It changed me completely, one abusive, cruel word or accusation at a time.

And then the wedding march resounded in my head and I crossed the threshold, changing my life with each painful step.

ALEXI'S & ASHLEY'S BIRTH'S—1988 & 1993

The honeymoon over, we settled into daily life. I was overwhelmed by the hold Roberto's DNA providers had on him and didn't understand why he jumped every time they called, even though we were married.
I tried quoting the Bible verse the priest had read during our wedding ceremony: Genesis 2:24, "Therefore man shall leave his father and his mother and shall become united and cleave to his wife, and they shall become one flesh," to no avail. That just made Roberto furious, which would result in him sulking for days. He found sulking or ignoring me amusing.

One night, we had plans to go to a new club in Pretoria. Roberto had taken his time and we were very late, so I suggested that we go on another night. The fact that I challenged Roberto's lateness made him really angry. He had no desire to be on time unless it involved his DNA providers. He insisted that we go. Firstly he drove like a maniac all the way to Pretoria, and then he proceeded to ignore me the entire evening.
Up until recently he would recount this story with glee finding the fact that he terrorised me with his driving and then proceeded to ignore me for hours hilarious. He didn't think there was anything wrong with his behaviour.

Our marriage has been defined by many sad, totally unnecessary incidents, generally involving Aradia and Lucifer's constant interfering in our lives, that have been gouged into my soul.

Sunday August the 25th of 1996 dawned bright and breezy. It was the first anniversary of Mr. Mc Cormack's passing and there was a memorial service at the church at which he had been the assistant minister. This involved a number of military dignitaries being present as well as many people involved with the organisations he had devoted countless hours to. I was looking forward to this service, as some form of closure, as the actual funeral had been like a circus. There had been hundreds and hundreds of people and all his biological family had been interested in was being in front and making a show of great emotion, even as though they had hardly seen him during his prime!

At that time we were living with my mother so my mom, Alexis, Ashley and I were up bright and early as we had agreed we'd leave the house by 8h15 so we could find parking and my mother could be outside to greet the many people attending. Many of these acquaintances she hadn't seen for the year since his passing. The past year had been a bizarre roller coaster ride packing up and either discarding or distributing the books, military memorabilia and personal belongings from Mr. Mc Cormack's three offices in their home.

Roberto was in one of his difficult moods. By 8 o'clock he hadn't even gotten out of bed. I was trying to be kindly persuasive reminding him of the importance of the service. He totally switched off and ignored me. Eventually we left at 9 o'clock, arriving 10 minutes after the actual service had started!

I was devastated and totally mortified that he could actually treat my mother with this total disrespect and disregard. My precious mother, now always gracious, just smiled and pretended everything was fine. My heart was broken. I never got my little bit of time to find closure!

Many months later I was to find out that Roberto was so difficult and ill mannered that day as Aradia had phoned him several times the previous day instructing him to attend some errand church service with her. This was because at the dreaded Friday night dinner Roberto had mentioned the Sunday memorial service and she was being blatantly spiteful and manipulative. True to form Roberto just couldn't tell me that Aradia was pressurizing him and he just didn't have the skills to deal with her. Instead he would just become totally unreasonable with me.

31

In 1993, the year Ashley was born, Lucifer's father passed away. I had organised a very successful fund raiser for Alexis's school. There was to be a general parents meeting where I was going to hand over the cheque and be thanked for my great effort. Roberto informed me on that afternoon that we had to be at the Catholic church to say "prayers" for the departed Grand-father that evening. Roberto had no recollection of this departed paternal Grand-father. The school meeting was at six o'clock. I felt comfortable that we could go to the school meeting and then onto the church by seven thirty—the normal time of any evening service. At the last minute Roberto informed me we had to be at the church by six fifteen. Feeling defeated and irritable, I was heavily pregnant, I went to the school and organised for someone else to do the presentation and accept the flowers on my behalf.

We sat in the cold, breezy church on the hard benches waiting endlessly for them to arrive. We couldn't phone them as there weren't cell phones at that time! Roberto refusing to leave in case they walked in and we weren't there. Eventually at eight fifteen they sauntered in, followed by the Priest who said a two minute prayer and we all left. I was livid asking why we had been instructed to be there so early. Lucifer laughed and said that Roberto had the time wrong! I was furious. Roberto questioned Aradia about the time. Eventually, with the tell tale glint of evil and triumph in her harsh eyes she admitted that Scorpio had told her about the presentation so she in turn told Roberto the wrong time!

Once again they had robbed me of ever being validated for anything.

Every single Friday night, without fail, we had to be at his DNA providers' house for dinner. We had to be there by six o'clock but rarely ate until after eight. These visits were extremely stressful. Aradia refused point blank to address me in English, so whenever I would go to the kitchen to help her, she would ignore me (and then tell Roberto that I was lazy and rude!).

I had been taught that when one goes for a meal at someone's house, it is polite to bring something to share. I started off by taking a cold drink or two. Aradia said that was rude, as it insinuated that she couldn't afford cold drinks.

I then took to taking along a homemade dessert. After the third time I stopped, as the dessert was always left untouched on the kitchen counter above the rubbish bin.

One Friday night I proudly made a standard salad of lettuce, tomato, cucumber, and onion, as Scorpio and Aradia mumbled between themselves. At dinner time I put the salad on the table, but Aradia looked at me and told Roberto in Portuguese, "Tell the *pades* that this is not how we make salad." She promptly stood up and tipped the entire salad into the garbage.

I had the urge to burst into tears and look to Roberto for solace, but I knew in my heart that would be the wrong thing to do, as I knew that he would only be furious with me. And so yet again I sat in silence as the humiliation and cruelty gouged another notch into my already scarred soul.

Before I started dating Roberto, any arrangements I ever had with friends were made at school and these arrangements were never broken. For instance we would arrange to meet on the number 32 bus that left the end of the main road at 9. At each stop one of the group of friends would get on the bus and we would then go to movies or go and walk around the City Centre. No-one ever didn't pitch or was late. There weren't cell phones and most of us were not at liberty to use the house phone. For the longest time we didn't even have a house phone that worked in the day! It was a shared line that only worked after six in the evening. So an arrangement was an arrangement. This cementing the respect and loyalty we had for each other.
Once we were married I was so proud to have my very own home phone! Fat lot of good that did me.
I often made arrangements to meet friends for coffee after the dreaded Friday evening dinner, but if Roberto asked if we could eat early, Aradia and Scorpio would make sure we dined late. That would then leave our friends waiting in vain for us. This happened regularly. So after a little while, I stopped making any arrangements to spare myself the humiliation and distress of dropping my friends and then having to try and explain that Roberto just refused to stand up to his DNA providers. Needless to say, in a very short space of time, any English friends we had quickly disappeared.

While in school, I had forged a bond with Nina, a Portuguese girl. She married Ricardo straight after leaving school, and the four of us began spending more and more time together. Nina was fun loving and genuine, and she accepted me for the person that I was. The four of us spent many happy hours together, even going away a few times together. She had a son the same month Abigail was born, and they were later also quite close for a time.

Nina was very different from all the other Portuguese girls; she didn't gossip, preferring a good laugh and the silly fun behaviour we often enjoyed. We spent many memorable evenings together, one I remember fondly was of going to a supper club where they had topless dancers. We were so innocent that this evening was our talking point for months afterwards.

We spent Christmas Eve of 1984 at Lucifer's uncle and aunt's house. Roberto offered to supply the wine. Off we went to the store, and Roberto encouraged me to get a bottle of Sputzendraght—a sweet wine I had tried previously and enjoyed. I was unsure, as I knew I'd only have half a glass at most. Roberto insisted and bought the wine. When dinner time came, Roberto asked what I would like to drink; obviously I said I'd have some of the wine he had purchased. It was still closed, as no one else liked sweet wine.

It was if the bottle of wine had blown an icy breath across the entire gathering. Firstly there was silence, and then his mean old uncle said that I was extremely rude to expect a bottle of wine to be opened just for me. Obviously everyone agreed wholeheartedly, while Roberto remained poised in midair, not sure of what to do. After a few minutes hesitation, he opened the wine and poured some for me while the entire table gabbled on about my selfish, rude behaviour. By this time, I understood Portuguese but had never told anyone, not even Roberto.

For a change, I felt validated by Roberto, but that feeling was short lived! For the rest of the evening, he totally ignored me and was noticeably annoyed with me. The next day, on Christmas morning, after much pleading from me, he accused me of being selfish, rude, and too demanding, while embarrassing him in front of his uncle. His reaction left me numb and wishing I could just go back to work.

At the end of February 1988, we discovered I was pregnant. I was overjoyed and just knew in my soul that I would be blessed with a precious little girl, who would be my solace and reason for carrying on for the rest of my life (once again, my sixth sense had kicked in).

We told Aradia and Lucifer with trepidation, and Lucifer's only response was "It not be nother shit girl like Scorpio give me. [Natasha had been born in December.] Marcell no know how do it like man. Look me I make two boys. I want boy for *familia* [family] name go on."

Speaking of that family, ironically, the intelligent bureaucracy in Portugal had made a mistake on Roberto's birth certificate. The DNA providers' surname starts with "De," but Roberto's official name is just "Abreu!" I've always known that Roberto really didn't belong in this cruel, demented family.

Then, with his crude, trademark vindictiveness, Lucifer continued, "This baby it make in mielie field like I make Roberto." His delight in his youthful sexual prowess made him puff up his chest while enjoying Aradia's distinct humiliation at being reminded that she wasn't the required and expected virgin bride.

My pregnancy progressed mostly uneventfully, although I did get far more severe migraines. On one particular Sunday, I felt really poorly and just wanted to stay at home alone with Roberto. That evening, seventeen-year-old Claude phoned and asked Roberto to go with him to the Portuguese club. I begged him to just stay home with me, to no avail. He promptly left, even though I was in tears while being violently ill. He returned after ten o'clock, which by our standards was late for a Sunday night. He then proceeded to sit in the lounge and drink an entire bottle of a rich liqueur, after which he became violently ill and threw up for hours.

I became hysterical and was sure that he was going to die of alcohol poisoning on our bathroom floor. Afterwards he was totally unapologetic, insisting that I wasn't going to control him ever.

The baby was due at the end of September, but on the last Sunday of August I started having contractions. I phoned my gynaecologist, who advised that I go to the hospital. I was lying on the examination bed when a Portuguese nurse sauntered and asked, "Is your sister-in-law Scorpio?"

"Why?" I asked, breathless from the last contraction.

"Cause we were in school together. You must be the *pades* she can't stand!"

Absolutely shocked I shouted, "Get out! Just get out!"

At that instant my gynaecologist walked in. "What's the problem, my little girl?" he asked very kindly. (I only weighed 40 kilos when I fell pregnant, so he always fondly referred to me as his little girl.)

Visibly distressed, I replied, "That nurse is friends with Roberto's sister. I can't expose myself to her."

Bless his soul, he was so kind and understanding. He simply instructed the nurse to leave and never to attend to me in any form or shape while saying to me, "I have never had a more modest patient than, you my little girl."

I just couldn't face the thought of one of Scorpio's friends seeing me totally exposed and then regaling her with a blow-by-blow account of my pain and distress. In my vast personal experience of Portuguese girls, that's exactly what she would have delighted in doing.

On 13 September 1988, my precious gift from God, Alexis, was born via C-section after she went into distress during my induced labour. Throughout the induction and subsequent labour, Roberto sat crunching on snacks while simultaneously eating greasy, smelly fried chicken, ignoring the fact that the smell of the fried chicken made me feel like throwing up. He only stopped when I was rushed to theatre for an emergency C-section.

Alexis weighed 2.3 kilos and was perfect. She was a textbook baby from the instant she was born. She just ate and slept. On the second morning after her birth, I just couldn't stop crying! In hindsight I had the baby blues, but there wasn't a lot of literature on the matter then, and I was totally ill informed. Roberto got irritated with me and just said, "You've only had a baby. Millions of women do it daily. Just stop it." The nurses just gave me a wide berth and expected me to sort myself out.

The hospital had a very strict policy that only the father and grandparents could visit the mother and only the father could see the baby. To my great anguish, Scorpio snuck into the maternity ward while I was feeding Alexis; she wanted to hold her. She revelled in my obvious distress, making it worse by pretending that the nurse was on the way. Scorpio, Marcell, and Rosa always enjoyed teasing me about being Little Miss Perfect who always obeyed the rules while they broke as many rules as possible. After that visit I had a shocking migraine, and my gynae moved me to a private room.

When Alexis was six weeks old, we went with Nina and Ricardo to a hot spring water resort for a few days. I made the very silly mistake of sitting on the floor of the communal change room to breast feed Alexis. When we returned, I really didn't feel well.

By the Friday I was very feverish and felt rather nauseous. However, being a Friday, we absolutely had to attend the dreaded Friday night dinner. I was too sick to eat, and the smell of the food turned my stomach. I sat quietly in the lounge with Alexis while everyone had dinner. Lucifer's uncle and aunt were there and made their feelings clear: they were disgusted that I didn't join them at the table, even though I was pale and had a high fever.

On Saturday I was admitted to the clinic with a severe kidney and bladder infection, where I remained for a week. I was gravely ill. None of Roberto's family visited me, as I had been too rude the previous Friday night!

Lucifer's youngest cousin—the youngest son of this rude, abrasive uncle—married an English woman later on in life. His parents weren't as hostile and cruel to her as Roberto's were to me, as they wouldn't dare to overplay their hand with their son. They did, however, make their displeasure known quite often until the English wife just refused to have anything further to do with them.

In 1996 their daughter was diagnosed with some form of leukaemia. On arriving home, totally over aught by this devastating diagnosis the only comment that Lucifer's aunt made to her daughter-in-law was "It you own fault she sick. You work, you *manina* (little girl) get sick! She die it you fault!" Need I say, that this Portuguese woman, also professed to be the most religious practising Catholic to ever have graced God's green earth.

Alexis started walking at ten months and speaking in full sentences at twelve months. She would listen to stories and then repeat them verbatim, as if she was reading, from fifteen months. She had snow white hair with huge sea blue eyes. Her skin was alabaster with rosy cheeks. Wherever we went, people were automatically drawn to her. She was kind, gentle, and very soft hearted. I never even raised my voice to her. She could speak and understand Portuguese fluently before she was two. However, when she was two and a half, after a particularly miserable visit with Roberto's DNA providers, Alexis pronounced, "I will never speak that language again. Daddy's family are too ugly to us." She never uttered another Portuguese word again, and if she understood anything that was said, she never let on.

Aradia looked after Natasha during the day while Scorpio was at work. Over my objections, Roberto insisted that Alexis stay with her as well. I was extremely unhappy with this arrangement. With trepidation and against my better judgement, Alexis started staying with Aradia in mid-1991.

The first disturbing incident happened one day while I was on my way to work; my mother and Mr. McCormack had given me a lift and we were driving behind Aradia, who was taking Scorpio to work, with Natasha and Alexis in the back seat (neither of them wearing seat belts, I might add). All of a sudden, we could see Natasha hit Alexis over the head. Alexis just bowed her head down, trying in vain to protect herself with her tiny arms. We began honking the horn frantically, and I was screaming out of the window. Aradia and Scorpio didn't even bat an eyelid. As soon as I got to work I phoned Roberto, and two hours later he managed to raise Aradia on her house phone. She blatantly denied the entire incident, insisting that my mother, Mr. McCormack, and I were lying!

To this day, Alexis can recall the unhappy times spent with Aradia and Natasha; her cousin delighted in making the most odious burps right in her face. She would then laugh, thinking her behaviour was very humorous and entertaining.

I begged Roberto to let me leave Alexis with my aunt, who had a day care centre. He absolutely refused. Fate then intervened. One day, I arrived to collect Alexis, and she had a huge graze on her delicate face with a pitch black, egg-sized lump on her forehead. Natasha had pushed her down the cement steps. Only then did Roberto agree to allow me to take Alexis to my aunt, where she was safe.

Like mother, like daughter: both big bullies.

My treasured little pixie, Ashley, was born on 22 December 1993, the twenty-ninth anniversary of my biological father's passing

By this time, our friendship with Nina and Ricardo had evaporated, like mist on a warm morning. She had stopped taking my phone calls and had stopped inviting Roberto and myself around to her home. I just couldn't fathom it out. Roberto insisted that I must have done something to upset Nina, but I knew otherwise. My suspicions were confirmed one Friday night when, with her signature snarl, Scorpio asked, "How's Nina?" I knew then she had something to do with Nina's suddenly ending our relationship. Roberto wouldn't believe me.

About ten years later, I bumped into Nina at a shop near my mother's home. She was decidedly uncomfortable. Then, totally flustered and visibly distressed, she blurted out, "I'm so very sorry I listened to Scorpio and dumped you. She kept telling me you said disgusting things about me. I'm so very sorry. I should never have believed or listened to her. You were the kindest, most honest, fun loving friend I've ever had. I'm truly sorry. Please forgive me." With that confession, she burst into tears, ran to her car, and sped off. I've never seen her again.

And so Scorpio had taken something else from me.

Ashley's birth was complicated; she was in intensive care for twenty-four hours and I couldn't take her home for four more days, due to severe yellow jaundice. She had to stay under ultraviolet lights at home for another five days. Each day the clinic sister came to prick her toe or finger to see how the jaundice was improving. I found this extremely stressful and disturbing, so my mother and Mr. McCormack would arrange to visit every time the clinic sister was there. From the instant

Mr. McCormack first held Ashley, there was an incredibly deep and sincere bond between them. They became inseparable.

Ashley was the antithesis of Alexis; she only slept a few hours a day. She started laughing heartily at six weeks on the way to my first check-up after her birth. This caused my mother to almost drive off the road, which caused great amusement every time we recounted the story. Everyone thought we were exaggerating until they heard Ashley's delightful, full-blown laughter.

Roberto's DNA providers didn't pay any attention to Ashley. Lucifer was totally disgusted that he now had four granddaughters. He saw this as a personal attack, a great travesty of justice, as he desperately wanted a grandson, as males were more important! As fate would have it he ended up with six granddaughters.

The dreaded Friday night dinners continued unabated. I begged Roberto to limit our attendance to only once or twice a month, to no avail. He insisted that we go every single week, without fail. From time to time, I still tried to do the right thing by taking along cold drinks, salad, or a dessert, but whatever I brought remained untouched and normally landed up in the garbage. A few times, I brought some steak or chicken. I found out later that these contributions were always given to the "kaffir girl" (no amount of me explaining that the lady who cleans one's home should be referred to by name instead of this slur made any difference).

Ashley was sickly and often, without any warning, would projectile vomit. It was scary at first, but then the paediatrician told me I was neurotic and plied her with antibiotics. There were numerous occasions that we learnt to take this vomiting in stride, much to the great shock of anyone else who was present. I would simply just pick her up, head for the nearest bathroom, change her, and return as if nothing had happened.

This continued unabated until October of 1995, when a mother at Ashley's preschool referred me to the kindest, most understanding ear, nose, and throat specialist. After examining Ashley for two minutes, he discovered the lymph nodes in her neck were causing the problem. The very next day, she was hospitalised and the lymph nodes were removed. No more projectile vomiting.

Ashley didn't speak. She used sign language, because her throat was always sore she couldn't speak. She had her tonsils removed at two and a half, and then in 1996 all her front teeth were removed because of taking too many antibiotics. Due to this, her jaw became inverted, so it was even more difficult for her to form words properly.

Ashley and her precious cousin Jessica became inordinately close and when-ever I couldn't understand her I would phone the then 12 year old Jessica to translate for me!

Through all of this, Roberto's DNA providers were totally unsympathetic, never once visiting her in hospital, often alluding to the notion that Ashley was mentally retarded and it was my fault—they claimed I had done something wrong during the pregnancy. Lucifer took great pride in being extremely cruel and mocking the way she spoke, making Ashley extremely frustrated. This caused immense tension, but Roberto said we should just ignore Lucifer, and his cruel ways as confronting him just made him do it more. Roberto still refused to stop the Friday night ritual.

In April of 1995, Ashley's beloved Papa was diagnosed with terminal cancer. It was truly devastating. As he became more ill, he couldn't come down the stairs. We would do everything possible to keep Ashley downstairs, but she would find a way to go upstairs and lay in the bed with him, often with her bald head lying on his severely distended tummy while his massive hand protectively cradled her head. It was the only time she was still.

Papa celebrated his last birthday with his six grandchildren from my mother's side, my sisters and me, our spouses, and my mother. His biological children were all too busy to be there, even though we all knew that this would be his final birthday.

At the time, Ashley was only sixteen months old, but she can still recount every detail of that evening. Her Papa sitting in the big arm chair with Aleen being the leader in the game follow the leader with Abigail, myself and the six kids following her ridiculous lead with Papa laughing uncontrollably. This is the memory that we have kept dear as after that night, his health went into a steady decline, as the ravages of cancer took him from a strapping goliath of a man to an emaciated, helpless being.

My precious mother often recounted this story of Ashley's great love and respect for her Papa. On returning from the specialist with the terminal cancer diagnosis very fresh in their hearts and minds, Ashley snuck upstairs, removed her Papa's shoes from his aching feet, and spent an hour rubbing his feet while kissing them every few minutes. Papa just sat still with tears streaming down his face. His love for this very different little girl was evident by the look of love and adoration in his sad eyes.

Ashley was effectively the 19th grand-child between my mother and Mr. Mc Cormack. There were also seven children, each with a spouse. Soon after his diagnosis it took a great deal of persuading by me and much ranting from my mother to persuade Papa to not leave his every worldly possession to Ashley. I shudder at the thought as to how his off spring would of reacted should that have happened!

Papa wrote Ashley a journal each day of his journey to the end of his long, illustrious life. He repeatedly said that he loved her more than life itself and knew she was destined for a great life. He reaffirmed a thousand times that she was special, gifted, and should never allow anyone to take that away from her.

Roberto's DNA providers were uninterested in any of our great emotional turmoil. They continued to cruelly taunt us and insist that we visit their house at inconvenient and inappropriate times.

With God's great grace and an answer to my prayers, we didn't go to the dreaded family dinner the Friday night Papa passed. Alexis held her Papa's hand as he passed, and for once, Ashley was fast asleep.
It was his constant praise of Ashley and his unconditional love for her that, I am sure, left her the least affected by the despicable behaviour of Roberto's DNA providers. Ashley is very outspoken, and she always says that she only had two grandparents: her precious Dassie (the name

she gave my mother), and her beloved Papa, who passed when she was little.

If she is questioned about her father's parents, she simply says, "Sharing DNA does not make anyone my grandparent. Grandparents are kind, loving, and understanding," and then she clams up!

CHRISTMAS EVE—2001

Christmas, Xmas, the festive season, yuletide—whatever you call this period of celebration, Christ's birth is a time when families gather together and all arguments and disagreements are forgotten. A time of being kind, gentle, loving, and tolerant, with a little bit of silly thrown in for good measure. Since we are celebrating the birth of our Saviour, we are conditioned to forget all ills. As I learnt the hard way, this was not so in the cruel, unrelenting realm I inhabit.

Christmas is critical in the Christian religion, as Jesus Christ and his birth were pivotal. Believing in Christ is what separates the Jews from the Christians. Most religions believe in a God; however, only Christians believe that Jesus Christ was God's son.

The birth of Christ is a magnificent, moving event revered by all Christians. Christians? What is a Christian? I find this title debatable. I need to constantly remind myself that saying twenty Hail Marys forgives all instantaneously. One can be forgiven for anything from hijacking, stealing, whatever, but especially for being incredibly spiteful and rude. All is forgiven after saying the all-forgiving Hail Marys!

Maybe I should commit a well thought out murder, recite the said Hail Mary's and carry on with a clear conscience. If only! I've considered this numerous times. Whom should I dispose of first? The thought of slowly bumping off this demented, cruel clan of DNA providers makes me giggle. I am in my 40's and am still I'm petrified of each one of Roberto's DNA providers. The thought has crossed my mind that perhaps I should attend some self help classes and confess, "Hello my name is Pippa I want to gain confidence to enable me to bump off my husband's DNA provider's!" To dream the impossible dream, to reach the unreachable goal . . . May God forgive these truly evil desires and thoughts.

In the Portuguese culture, Christmas is generally celebrated on Christmas Eve with a family dinner and then the sharing of gifts at midnight. This practise suited us well, as we could then spend Christmas Day with my family, thereby avoiding any uncomfortable decisions.

In 2001, to our horror, Roberto announced that dinner would be at Claude and Morrisa's duplex, instead of at Lucifer and Aradia's house. I didn't like the sound of this. My entire being instantly went into knots, and I knew within the pit of my being that this could only spell disaster. However, who was I to challenge any autocratic decision? No one ever dared challenge Morrisa, who was totally controlling, domineering, and quite frankly frightening. In all the years I have known her, I can count the number of times I've seen her smile, including on her wedding day. Her demeanour commanded compliance and submission. Always.

My precious girls and I laugh for everything. I have, over the years, of intense discrimination and cruelty learnt, and have taught my precious girls, to find the silver lining in every cloud. So this very stern demeanour makes us very nervous, and hyper sensitive thus making us laugh even more.

Roberto was advised that the *pades* (I could surely hear the faint addition of "*puta*") must not, under any circumstances, bring anything to eat. Everyone knew I could not cook, and even if I brought anything edible, no one would touch it anyway. I was, however, instructed to bring fifteen cold drinks! A detailed list is provided, for eleven people (three being children).

For good measure I packed in a few normal tea bags as they only ever have Rooibos tea, which at the best of times makes me feel nauseous. I'm sure, should I have forced the Rooibos tea down my very constricted throat under very stressful circumstances, as beady eyes watched my every pained sip, I would have projectile vomited. Chaos would have ensued as my precious girls collapsed and me choked to death. While

45

the demented, cruel DNA providers stood by and watched our demise, their immense glee uncontained.

My precious girls and I went shopping and chose a delightful fairy ornament for Polly, a beautiful glass vase for Claude and Morrisa, and an assortment of lotions and potions for Aradia (Roberto insisted that this was the only gift we must ever buy her, and we always complied). We also bought the standard expensive shirt from Woolworths for Lucifer, even though we have never seen him wear any shirt we've bought him.

My precious girls and I spent many fun-filled hours painstakingly wrapping each gift and enclosing them with bows, thereby ensuring that the joy and sense of giving, which we think is very Christmassy, expresses our delight in giving freely; we were ready to enjoy Christmas.

We had a long and chequered history of gift receiving with Claude and Morrisa. Ever since she weaselled her way onto the scene, my precious girls have never received a single gift for either their birthday or Christmas from Claude and Morrisa. Each time, with her deadpan face, she would advise us that "I forgot your gift in the cupboard under the stairs." Eventually, the girls and I came to poke fun at the size of this elusive cupboard. We were sure it soon was bursting at the seams. I constantly assured them that they didn't need gifts that were given with any kind of grudge. It was far better to go without and know what you received from others were gifts that were given with love. Be it a boiled sweet or a million dollars.

We were advised that dinner would be precisely at eight o'clock. At six, we were about thirty minutes away; for once we would be on time and not admonished for our tardiness. Or so we thought.

Just then Roberto's phone rang; it was Claude. "Why are you late?" No hello, how is your long drive going, or how are you, just why are you late?

"Late? *Senora* [Roberto *never* called Aradia "Mae" or "Mom"] said dinner is at eight."

"Well, any decent person knows that you always arrive two hours before dinner for the pre-dinner schedule."

Roberto raised his eyebrow and a huge smile crept across his face; my precious girls and I have to stuff our hands into our mouths to smother our hysterics. "Pre-dinner schedule?" Roberto asked, shocked. "What's that?"

Claude was obviously furious, and we could hear Morrisa in the background, saying, "You know since Roberto has been involved with those people [people who aren't Portuguese], he has lost all sense of etiquette." (Am I mad or have I been "involved" with this cruel, demented DNA clan since 1980, whereas she only came in 1994?) There was a huge sigh from Claude. "What time exactly will you be here?"

In the Holy Catholic Mass there is a mantra: "Lord have mercy, God have mercy, Christ have mercy." I repeated this out loud, and then we all, including Roberto, dissolved, unable to contain our absolute mirth at the ridiculousness of Morrisa's statement. She was so very self-absorbed and such a control freak.

I then called upon God's great mercy again as we proceeded to get terribly lost. My insane behaviour only made matters worse. By this time, our nerves were shredded, and we dreaded what was in store for this Christmas Eve.

When we finally arrived, I raised my outstretched arms heavenward and said with intense emotion, "Hallelujah! Praise God!" This always ensured that we would enter visibly laughing (a real crime against humanity). I am sure when I pass, I will be on a one-way ticket to hell!

We arrived at around six forty were summarily admonished by Morrisa's stare for being late and messing up the pre-dinner schedule. We placed the gifts under the tree as she commented contemptuously, "All wrapping and no substance, I suppose."

We lugged the required fifteen cold drinks into the kitchen. Morrisa then promptly divided the cold drinks into two groups and stored one group in the famous cupboard under the stairs. To Roberto's horrified glance, Ashley nearly fell over, trying to see the promised stack of gifts. Her little mind obviously thinking it must be a humungous cupboard to fit all the gifts and now those cold drinks. We, in the meantime, made ourselves comfortable in the lounge.

Morrisa positioned herself in the centre of the lounge, dwarfing us all, and instructed, "We will *all* be going for a walk around the complex," in a voice that defied challenge.

Both my precious girls poked me, and I looked at Roberto and said casually, "We'll just wait here and chat."

As though we weren't even present, Morrisa began whispering to Claude. I could lip read perfectly: "There is no way those people are staying in my house without me here."

"Why don't you want us to stay here without you?" I asked, extremely shocked.

Morrisa was visibly annoyed that I knew exactly what she had said; she was saved by Aradia, who jumped to her defence and said in Portuguese to Roberto, "These people, they have no manners, first they are late [um, Roberto wasn't late as well?]; when at someone's house, you have to do exactly as they say, blah blah blah."

My precious girls and I saw Roberto's entire demeanour change—a sure sign of trouble. We all proceeded to go on the scheduled walk, avoiding another evening of being totally ignored and humiliated by Roberto.

We pretended to be prisoners of war, being frog marched from one destination to another by a member of the Third Reich, marching, terrified, into the unknown, ever only expecting the worst. Our silly little joke eased our tension, but sadly, that was exactly how we were made to feel.

We were terrified of infuriating Roberto, as otherwise our family gathering the next day would be purgatory. Roberto would be sure to throw one of his tantrums; besides being extremely humiliating for us, it was devastatingly hurtful.

When we returned to the duplex, Morrisa once again commanded, "Now for half an hour we will *all* watch home videos of Polly."

My precious girls and I sat close together and chatted quietly. Inevitably, I could feel disgusted eyes boring into us. Roberto nudged me and said to be quiet.

"Why?" I asked. "We are talking quietly about colours for the girls' bedrooms and not disturbing anyone."

Roberto responded desperately, "Well, we have to listen to Polly's videos."

"Why?" I repeated. "We don't have to be forced to watch anything"

Roberto coloured immediately. Aradia responded, her brash, ear-piercing voice cutting into the uncomfortable silence, "You Morrisa's *casa* [house], you make like she say you, those [my precious girls] look Polly, she the clever, she the pretty."

My heart stopped. I caught my breath, my instinct being to grab both my precious girls and run out of that hurtful, demeaning situation.

How can a supposed grandmother blatantly insult two delightful, generous, kind, pretty young girls?

Roberto glared at me, obviously fearing the worst, and very quietly uttered, "Just leave it and listen. It's easier."

My precious girls understood; they both squeezed my legs, silently letting me know they would rather comply than have ugliness all evening. "Easier" to let the daughters you supposedly adore and respect be insulted so blatantly. I'm left seething and, once again, totally humiliated.

I retreated into my own special place, where I admonished myself for being in this unhealthy, cruel situation, for being so naïve and trusting, believing that when I converted to Catholicism and married Roberto, his family's attitude towards me would change.

My entire life, I had dreamed of a happy family who spoke kindly to one another, of a father who would love and guide me. I didn't have it while growing up, so I dreamed of getting it when I got married. In hindsight, with my self-esteem in tatters, my soul destroyed, all the self-help gurus were correct. You cannot change "your man" once you are married. The ground rules must be laid way before the wedding.

As I have learned, you and you alone set the bar for how your partner will treat you. It is your own responsibility to ensure that your partner knows what is acceptable and what is not. That's all fine and well in theory, but practically, when you don't have any self-esteem and are so sure no one will ever really love and respect you, the focus blurs.

Each time your innermost being is scared, seared by hatefulness and discrimination, you are sure it will be the last. It took me twenty-nine long years to admit to myself that unless I absolutely put my foot down and demanded complete change, this demeaning, controlling, soul-destroying behaviour would continue.

At precisely seven thirty, the videos stopped. "Now you people can chat," Morrisa commanded with relish, a sense of power in her crude voice. Her demeanour was hateful. At precisely eight, we were ordered to the table. The meal was laid out on a separate counter. After the superficial grace was said (just another charade of deep Christianity), we proceeded to serve.

My precious girls and I hung back; Roberto said he would help the girls serve, as they were clearly very uncomfortable. He took a chicken leg for Ashley and a breast with two prawns for Alexis; with her hands on her hips, Morrisa scolded, "What are you people doing? You people know nothing."
What was with the excessive use of "you people" tonight? "You people" was a derogatory term, often used as a general insult, or in a condescending manner, driving the admonished insane.

With her arms outstretched and rolling her eyes, Morrisa explained, speaking extremely slowly and enunciating each word very carefully (I'm not sure if this was for our benefit or to make sure that Roberto's DNA providers understood), "It is etiquette to start with salad only, then the chicken and vegetables, and then only when everyone is finished to maybe have one or two prawns."
(Secretively, I wondered if Morrisa had been reading the dictionary, as her command of the English language was normally very restricted). There were, however, a copious amount of prawns.

That brash, ear-piercing voice brought me back from my wondering; she was still carrying on about these pades who knew nothing and had no manners. Flabbergasted and furious, in utter frustration, I served twenty prawns for myself while smiling at my precious girls. "Wench," I slurred, grabbing five more prawns with my hand and tossing them onto Alexis's plate. "Let's chow down."

We took our seats, with everyone glaring at us. Roberto desperately tried to divert the conversation to something about building. We started eating, chatting amongst ourselves as always. Within two minutes, we heard another harsh command: "This tablecloth is extremely expensive. No messing on it anyone" An accusatory finger, accompanied by accusing glares, was directed ominously at the three pades.

The prawns were delicious. Anarchy diverted, we continued enjoying our meal as though there were only the three of us, while "those people" were speaking Portuguese, with ugly gossip and unkindness the only order of the conversation.

Roberto offered us drinks. My precious girls ask for cream soda; we had brought three bottles of the treat as part of our contribution to the meal.

Instantaneously, Morrisa scolded, "No, I think not! Polly loves cream soda, so it is only for her."

She's just three; how much cream soda can she drink? I protested that I had brought plenty.

"No, the other two bottles are for during the week!" Morrisa commanded, in a voice that ensured no one would challenge her.

My precious girls and I looked at one another and just smiled. What a bunch of rude, cruel people. In that look, my precious girls knew that no matter what, I'd never put them through this again. No matter what. I got up and poured us water from the tap. Why make such an issue? Lord have mercy, God have mercy, Christ have mercy.

All of a sudden there was a crash, and Lucifer dropped his overfilled red wine glass (a few too many on the lips already today, I imagined). The gods were protesting. The red wine splashed directly onto the prized tablecloth. I breathed a sigh of relief, as for once it wasn't the pades who were the centre of unwelcome, harsh scrutiny. My precious girls and I silently loved the mayhem that ensued, their delight palpable as I was kicked on both ankles. During the mayhem which ensued, we committed the cardinal sin of serving ourselves seconds, which we thoroughly enjoyed.

After dinner was over, we were advised that dessert would not be served until after presents were opened at midnight. We waited patiently, and then hickory dickory dock, the mouse ran up the clock, the clock struck twelve, and . . . I wished the mouse only ran down!

There were copious amounts of gifts for Polly. Aradia had formally instructed Roberto not to bring any of our gifts for our precious girls, as Claude and Morrisa didn't want Polly to feel they received more than her. Fair deal, we thought, and as always, we complied. So there we sat, Polly with a humungous pile of gifts, ripping open each one and then discarding it without so much as a thank you or a second glance.

When she opened the fairy ornament we had so lovingly chosen, she just dropped it on the floor. My precious girls only received an envelope with a little cash from Roberto's DNA providers. Polly received four expensive, nicely wrapped gifts from them alone. True to form, my precious girls didn't receive anything from Claude and Morrisa. What to do? They couldn't use the famous cupboard as an excuse.

My precious pixie Ashley, in all her innocence, asked, "Mom, why can't they just get all the presents out of the cupboard under the stairs, cause then my sissy and I can have them?" The silence was deafening. "Don't lie, it will come back to bite you in the bum" crossed my mind, as well as "out of the mouths of babes."

Just then, Lucifer grunted and threw his expensive shirt on the floor, exclaiming with pride, "Pippa and Roberto, we all no think bout you—ha ha ha—you get nothing." His personal joke was funny to him alone, as always.

I recall the Christmas of 2001 when Polly was 6 and Tracy 2. Eventually it is present opening time after what could have been called an uneventful Christmas Eve dinner, Aradia and Lucifers house, with minimal snipes and barbs.

My precious girls and I were cocooned in our own little world eager to spend Christmas day with their true family. As my precious girls and I have well established, sharing DNA doesn't automatically make you a Mother, Father, Sister, Brother, cousin or anything for that matter. What makes you family is your actions and the amount of dignity, love and respect afforded your fellow human beings.

There are countless verses in the Bible where Mother's are told to teach their children to be kind, loving and respectful, just as she is, by setting a good example. So Aradia—the greatest Christian to ever have graced the earth, missed this vital teaching somewhere.

As from April 1980 she has constantly pitted one sibling against the other, alienating Roberto and causing incredible hatred and untold heartache between them, him and me.

Roberto and I had chosen out a delightful shop till for Ashley. It had paper money, coins, even a credit card, a microphone that you could make store announcements over and a cash drawer that went ping. Alexis was eager to play with her sissy with this delightful new toy. Ashley, carefully opened the wrapping commenting on each picture of Father Christmas. Recalling happily how her beloved Papa had a moustache like that, ears like that. She made us smile as yes he did have big ears! Especially when he passed, Ashley was not even two, remembered him being skin and bones which made his ears appear huge! However his huge well manicured handle bar moustache was impeccable, even as he was carried away by the undertakers.
Ashley and Alexis relished every moment of the precise gift opening and eventually produced the delightful till, which we still have today

Polly received a huge kitchen set standing 1 metre tall, with a stove, all the utensils, together with several smaller parcels filled with everything one could ever need in a kitchen. Ashley's face lit up, running the credit card through the machine and announcing "next customer please" with utter delight. My heart was warm and content. As usual my little Pixie afforded me immense pleasure.

Polly launched her rather large self at Ashley and grabbed the precious till screaming "this is mine as well leave go you big bully". Ashley was knocked flat onto her skinny bottom while Alexis lost her balance and fell into my lap. Bully! My precious girls are both kind, gentle and caring. Immediately tears started flowing down Alexis' ashen face while Ashley just staring in utter shock. I got up and grab the till from a sullen faced Polly admonishing "If anyone is a bully it's you".

I have silently taken an enormous amount of abuse and cruelty from this family, but don't abuse my precious girls. Instantly the entire family surrounds Polly loving her," never mind we have one of those exact tills in the cupboard at home (the famous cupboard under the stairs), we were going to give it to you in the morning. Never mind if your selfish cousin won't share with a younger cousin. We all know those people are selfish and spiteful" Morrisa almost whispers in a very condescending voice. Look at the pot calling the kettle black!

Our shocked huddle is interrupted with the brash, ear piercing voice of Aradia who admonished Roberto in Portuguese for giving Ashley the till then. For once Roberto came to our defence and we leave. The till very firmly under my arm, while Claude asked Roberto, in a very hushed tone, where we had bought the delightful till!
After all the gifts were opened, in 2004, Morrisa glared at my precious girls and held out a black bag to them. "Clean up," she commanded.

Normally, I was petrified of each one of these cruel, demented DNA providers; I generally complied with their demands, making no comment when they were openly nasty and condescending.

I have always taken the bizarre stand that I am the better person, the path of least resistance—the story of my life. You have heard of the old adage, sticks and stones may break my bones but words will never harm me. I beg to differ. As I have discovered and still carry in my broken heart words do harm. More than I will ever be able to explain. A black eye heals but insults and cruel words harm a lot forming deep gauged in scars that develop into festering scars, never to heal, brought to the fore at the most inopportune moments.
However, to blatantly humiliate and take advantage of my precious girls was another thing altogether. I gave them a look that they instantly understood. They turned, smiled lovingly at their father, and said, "Let's go, Dad. We have a surprise for you at home" (meaning my mother's home, where we were staying).
I leaned forward, took a huge breath, and handed the bag to Polly, saying, "You've made a dreadful mess, lovey; you should clean up."

With pounding heart and dry mouth, I awaited an outburst from Morrisa and Aradia. My precious girls grabbed their father's arms and propelled him towards the door, with me in hot pursuit. All smiles and delight, we eagerly said good night. In our eagerness to escape, we forgot to protect our breasts, so each of us got an unwelcomed, disgusting, definitely creepy chest rub from Lucifer. His satisfaction of blind siding us with his perversion was obvious. Lucifer had taken to rubbing his chest against our breasts, even the undeveloped breast of my precious daughters, each time he greeted us.

As we drove off into the warm night, a shooting star burst into sight; we all watched as it lit up the sky, signalling the start of the true Christian birth of Christ. A delightful day would be filled with love, laughter, kindness, and respect. We would be sharing the birthday of Christ with family—some we share DNA with, some we don't, but they were all our family in every sense of the word.

Christmas with our family was delightful. In this case, all that glittered was gold. This Christmas, there were twenty-two people at Aleen's home. Our entire immediate family, including Jessica's boyfriend, a friend of theirs, Bruce's mother, and Avis, a family friend.

Instead of the costly indulgence of buying a gift for each person, we each chose one name, with a preset limit, and then buy an appropriate gift for that person. We would write a rhyme for the person to guess who the gift was from. This proved to be great fun, with much laughter and imaginations running riot.
Ashley was totally enthralled with Harry Potter, and having chosen her cousin Kevin, she bought him some aftershave and hid it in a cauldron filled with worms and snakes, with a powder puff ball for smoke. Her delight was immense. Her much older cousin humoured her excitement by eating copious amounts of sour, already licked worms, performing three silly forfeits for guessing wrong. We all enjoyed the spectacle. This teenager gentle and kind while showing unconditional love for his little cousin. Ashley adored him, so very proud to have tricked him! Now that is the true spirit of Christmas!

Shaun presented Roberto's gift; he flamboyantly sauntered in, shirtless, carrying a pizza box and singing a song about being at a rock concert. The gift was a CD by Queen, and Roberto's pure enjoyment was plastered openly over his sunny face. What a huge change from twelve hours previously.

My precious mother, ever the gracious old dame, was presented with a fake gloved hand carrying a silk evening bag. Her rhyme dignified and beautiful. She gratefully accepted the standard Estee Lauder base that she adored and which always lasted just 365 days.

After much laughter, silliness, and general fun, we enjoyed a delectable lunch. Each of us had provided a delectable dish or two, and we ate as we wished. Some ate later, as there were no rules, schedules, or pressure.

My precious girls and I sat very close together; however, this time it was not for protection and comfort, but in quiet relaxation as we watched Roberto laugh and joke around. We were enthralled by the deep meaningful relationship he had with his nieces, nephews, and their partners. There was absolutely no DNA shared between them, but they loved their special uncle in every sense of the word.

Eventually, we all retired, content, relaxed, surrounded by love and happiness. God does listen. Christmas day was fulfilling, delightful, with no stern unkind words spoken, no disagreements.

EASTER—OUR HOME—2003

The holiest of holy events in the Catholic calendar is Easter, where the crucifixion and resurrection of God's Almighty Son is celebrated with much pomp and ceremony. The Easter celebration is preceded by forty days of Lent. This is supposed to be a time of fasting and penitence from Ash Wednesday to Holy Saturday. A time of making sacrifices that truly show you are repentant for your sins and misdemeanours. A time when Christians around the world recall and emulate God's supreme generosity. A time when they recall God's selfless generosity of spirit when he gave his only begotten Son, so that we may have everlasting life. A time when we should really show our commitment to God and his commandments. A time of living as true Christians by being kind, generous, and all forgiving. Once again, this is not so in the realm of "Roman Catholic Christianity" that I inhabit!

Personally, I believe that one can live a life as a true Christian without making any grand gestures by shouting your Christianity from the roof tops. I believe that the way you live your life and conduct yourself, all year round, should make it clear to everyone you deal with that you are a God-fearing Christian. However, Roberto's entire DNA clan makes a huge issue of their grand gestures during Lent; they would make a huge hullabaloo of giving up Coke, or forgoing green beans for forty days, but then continue to be mean, spiritually and practically, as well as spiteful and discriminatory!

Easter Sunday of 2003 dawned with the usual sense of trepidation I'd get when the DNA providers are set to arrive. My dear mother was scurrying around, trying to keep me calm. A million times, I would try to come up with an answer as to why the DNA providers insisted on coming here to visit. It was quite apparent from their behaviour that they absolutely detested anything I ever cooked and complained from the instant they arrived until the instant they left. Often, when my precious girls and I would huddle together, contemplating this travesty of justice, Alexis would say she truly believed that they did it just to terrorise us. "Have you seen the delight in Aradia's eyes when Dad starts fighting with you in front of them?" she'd say. "Have you seen the look of triumph that passes between Aradia and Lucifer when Dad starts ignoring you when they are here?"

On this balmy Easter Sunday, Roberto was in our vast garden, finishing off the exciting Easter egg hunt he had planned. Roberto usually treated me despicably and has been totally disloyal and downright cruel, but when it came to things like Easter egg hunts for his daughters, he always went the extra mile and put his all into making them unforgettable. He even made detailed maps with burnt edges, like old pirate's maps. One clue leads to another, with rhymes and songs making up the clues. My precious girls were extremely excited.

After the local Sunday morning service, the dreaded DNA providers arrived, with Morrisa's mother and father in tow (two extras which had not been relayed to me). The usual terse greetings followed, and I swept Ashley up into my arms to avoid Lucifer's trademark perverted chest rub. The clan trudged in, laden with pots, pans, and containers filled with Portuguese food, even though I had spent two days preparing a scrumptious meal fit for royalty. I seemed to have forgotten that the Portuguese are the only people in the universe who can cook.

Polly sauntered in, carrying a bag filled with huge, brightly covered Easter eggs, including an extremely elaborate solid chocolate egg embellished with marzipan. In her other greedy hand, she clutched a brand new Barbie doll as well as an envelope containing R300-00, which was a lot of cash for a little girl, (I sneaked a peak while everyone was dishing up). Polly delightedly let everyone know that these gifts were from Aradia and Lucifer. True to form, my precious girls each received a much smaller envelope from Aradia and Lucifer, and no gifts. Claude mumbled lamely that their gifts for my precious girls had been forgotten in the now infamous cupboard under the stairs, promising to hand them over the "next time we see you!"

Polly then sent Claude to the car to haul in a bag full of clothes and stationery she had received from her grandparents and proceeded to lay all the colourful paints, pens, and stickers out on the coffee table for everyone to inspect. Roberto had insisted that we buy a lovely porcelain figurine for Polly, which she promptly discarded, without any hint of recognition or thanks.

Without any further waste of time, the Easter egg hunt was on. Roberto proudly handed out the maps and clues. My precious girls were excitedly following the map and shrieking in pure delight when they discovered a hidden treasure. Polly proceeded to scream and cry, accusing them of cheating. To calm her down, Claude began running around the garden, grabbing any eggs in sight and filling a bag for her, ruining many of the hiding places pointed to by Roberto's clues. The look of utter dismay was clearly plastered across his face. True to form, he didn't dare comment on this destructive, despicable behaviour.

Defeated, Roberto announced that Aradia wanted to eat immediately. We trudged inside for lunch. My entire delectable meal was left untouched by the DNA providers. I noticed a cloud pass over my precious mother's normally congenial face while she proceeded to make a big fuss over my delectable spread.

When lunch was over, Lucifer and Aradia announced that they had to leave immediately. For some bizarre reason, my mother was getting a lift back home with them, a situation that had never occurred before.

My precious girls went into Ashley's room to help their Gran gather her baggage. While there, my mom remembered that she had brought each of them a token Easter gift. She gave them each a butterfly mobile, made by the young inhabitants of a girls' home at which she volunteered. With great pride, she explained to my precious girls that the mobiles were made from discarded plastic milk bottles. She was delighted to explain that the beads used on the mobiles were beads we had sent to the home during one of our clean-outs.

Our home is filled with small ornaments made from any recyclable material imaginable. We even have Christmas "angels" made from gold painted pasta—they are beyond kitsch! But we take them out, reluctantly, every year and adorn our wooden, hand carved decorated tree with these strange looking hanging ornaments. Why, you ask? These mobiles were made with great pride and a sense of achievement by young girls who had survived the most horrendous circumstances and were now trying to rebuild their shattered lives in the girls' homes. My mother would buy and distribute these items to assist the home in their fundraising endeavours.

My precious girls were delighted with their gifts and proceeded to carry her bags to Aradia and Lucifer's car. We said our good-byes to my mother inside, rather than face the DNA providers at the car.
I felt somewhat bewildered as the car pulled off. The visit had passed with relative calm and no huge injustices, but I had an intense feeling of unease in the pit of my stomach. Silently, I prayed that the journey to Johannesburg would be incident free.

I busied myself with cleaning up while constantly praying, as the sense of dread mounted considerably as time passed. Eventually, my mother phoned to say she had arrived. I breathed a sigh of relief and confided my sense of discord and dread. Hesitantly, she told me that not five minutes into the journey, the car stopped abruptly at a garage cafe, and with much shaking of heads and raised voices, Aradia went in and bought Polly a copious amount of sweets; she also used the ATM and presented Polly with R200-00. Hesitantly, my mother confided that she felt very uneasy and that the upset seemed to have something to do with her. For the first time in the twenty-one years that Roberto and I had been together, my mother acknowledged that Aradia and Lucifer had an evil aura about them.

I questioned Roberto to see if he had heard from any of his DNA providers. He hadn't; they seldom phoned when they arrived back anyway. I was still filled with a sense of dread, and before falling asleep I begged God to calm me.

The sense of dread intensified, and by Tuesday afternoon, I was like a cat on a hot tin roof. When Roberto arrived home from work, I could see that my precious girls and I were in for a very rough time. His eyes were minuscule pinpricks, and the furrow between his eyes was deep.

"Your darling, saintly mother," he said sarcastically, "is selfish and cruel."

Dumbfounded, I asked, "Why?"

"How can she give Alexis and Ashley gifts in front of Polly while totally ignoring the poor child? That is cruel and selfish. It was Easter. You are supposed to be fair to everyone, and she was so cruel. Blah blah . . ."

I switch off while motioning to my precious girls to go through to spare them this tirade. Eventually I established that Polly had peeped through the half-closed bedroom door and saw my mother give the girls the mobiles; according to Roberto, she was "devastated and deeply hurt at being so blatantly left out!" He added, "My mother says your wonderful mother is the furthest thing from a Christian she has ever seen!"

My instinct was to retaliate and say, "Look at the pot calling the kettle black." But I remained silent.

It did not matter that I reminded Roberto that Polly had arrived here laden with gifts, which she blatantly showed off with much relish. The fact that our daughters had received a paltry R100-00 each from Lucifer and Aradia went unnoticed. The fact that the mobiles had been bought on the spur of the moment went unnoticed. The fact that Polly was not related to my mother in any way went unnoticed. The fact that Polly peeped around the almost closed door went unnoticed.

So there ended the generosity of spirit of our Easter. Once again the "pades" were condemned to the depths of hell, while the saintly, generous, and fair "Christian" Portuguese vented all their aggression and hatred upon us.

Unashamedly, for the next few years, I manipulated Roberto's work schedule so that he was on call each Easter weekend, ensuring that we couldn't visit his DNA providers and they couldn't come to see us!

Easter Sunday of 2006 saw us driving in tense silence through to Johannesburg for dinner with Aradia and Lucifer. The redeeming factor being that Easter Monday was to be held at Aleen's home and Abigail's home. Dinner passed quickly and with minimum conversation. Roberto was clearly relieved when it was over.

Easter Monday dawned warm and sunny, with a delectable breakfast expertly prepared by Bruce. It was heart-warming to have our entire immediate family together with all the cousins having come together to join us. We were also joined by Bruce's mother and his brother Anton and his wife Sylvia; tragically, they had lost their daughter in a hijacking the previous February.

After enjoying the easy fellowship of a jovial breakfast, everyone gathered for an Easter egg hunt. We divided into two groups, captained by the two Grannies.

Shaun claims to be agnostic and Kevin claims to be an atheist. We have had many heated and interesting debates. However, today, showing their respect for the two Grannies, they set up the most interesting, intricate Easter egg hunt based on bible verses. That two young men, both who have had their own hurdles to climb and have both had their fair share of ups and downs should put all that aside and show their generosity of spirit in taking the time to arrange something that neither of them believed in, warmed me to my core.

Anton was on my team. Since his precious daughter's untimely death, he had become morose and totally uncommunicative. I had to tease him kindly and threaten him with no dessert just to get him to participate. After much running, pushing, and shoving and general hilarity between the teams, he slowly started to get involved. Suddenly, and to everyone's astonishment, he hoisted Ashley high above his head to grab a well-hidden egg from a tree. At that moment, my eyes locked with Bruce; his glistened with gratitude that his lost brother seemed to have emerged from his darkness, at least for a little while.

After the hunt was over—won, I must proudly say, by my team—Anton wandered over to me, and with his eyes filled with tears, he said softly, "Your family is kind and generous. I felt my heart beat for the first time since it stopped last February."

I engulfed him in a tight, all-consuming hug while he sobbed from the depths of his being, something he had battled to do since his daughter had passed on.

Now that was the spirit of remembering God's great generosity in giving his son for our sins. None of us went to church that Easter, none of us had given up anything for Lent, but we were all kind, generous, and considerate. In my humble opinion, that is the true mark of Christian behaviour. No grand proclamations. No hullabaloo about our commendable "Christian" behaviour. Just genuine, quiet generosity of spirit.

As usual, as our family gathering drew to a close, Roberto could be found surrounded by his nephews and nieces, all vying for his attention, hanging on his every word. Would there ever be even a semblance of this harmony and generosity when we were with his DNA providers?

CHRISTMAS—2004

Every year the run-up to Christmas was really stressful. The thought of spending Christmas Eve with Roberto's DNA providers would make me sick to my stomach. So for Christmas 2004, I refused point blank to have Christmas anywhere but at our home, not only for my own sanity but also for my precious girls' protection. Months before, I started laying the plans with my sisters and my precious mother, stupidly thinking that this year would be free of the demented, cruel DNA providers! My precious girls and I revelled in our coup and started planning this exciting event months in advance. God is good, and he heard our pleas.

Christmas with our family was always delightful, fun, and relaxed.

We had a lovely home; every room was painted a different vibrant colour. I subconsciously chose these warm, inviting, uplifting colours to mask the utter disappointment I felt in myself for allowing this demented family to ruin such a huge chunk of my existence. On several occasions, friends would make themselves comfortable on my kitchen floor, sit on the green lounge couch, or prostrate themselves on the girls' bedroom floors and announce with warmth and wonderment, "This is the loveliest, kindest home I've ever been in." I loved this! This compliment also came from boys who hailed from extremely wealthy homes, where everything was of the very best (unlike our home, with the mishmash of furnishings, as well as photos, chimes, fairies, and angels that adorn our ceilings, walls, and surfaces).

We had a huge garden which was inhabited by our brood of beloved dogs (we had as many as thirteen), Alexis's cat Zina (who was a magnificent, huge grey and white feline specimen), two tortoises, and two bearded dragons, as well as an assorted cacophony of birds which I loved watching and who insisted on waking me every morning.

We also had a large pool that afforded us much pleasure. The girls and I would take a dip as the sun dipped behind the horizon, or go for a late night swim with friends, or just enjoy the lazy, quiet pleasure on any God-given summer day.

Our well-planned Christmas celebration of 2004 was getting nearer; with two weeks to go, one day Roberto came home with the telltale pinprick eye and a deep furrow between his eyes. My heart stopped. Instinctively, I knew it was Christmas drama and awaited the onslaught. Without any consultation, he announced that his demented DNA providers, together with Claude, Morrisa, Polly, and Tracy, would be having Christmas Eve dinner at our home, spend the night, and then leave early in the morning, before all our family arrived.

I had one of two choices. I could try to change this decision, but I knew this wouldn't work; it would only make the demented DNA providers more adamant at ruining our plans and being inordinately cruel, ensuring a truly black Christmas for myself and my precious girls. This all in true devout Christian Christmas spirit! Or I could agree and focus on the morning of the 25th, eagerly awaiting the arrival of the cavalry to support us, transporting me and my precious girls to a loving, kind, relaxed place. I firmly decided on the latter.

Our family always chose one person to buy a gift for, and I eagerly suggested that Roberto propose this fun, inexpensive gift giving tradition to the demented family. They vehemently declined this as a very stupid idea—only stingy, uneducated people would not give each person a gift (never mind that Morrisa and Claude had never given any of us a gift).

As usual, Roberto was informed that the pades must not, under any circumstances, cook anything, as everyone knew I was totally incapable of ever producing anything edible. This arrangement suited me perfectly, as I could concentrate on planning and cooking for the 25th. On the morning of the 24th, I busied myself in the kitchen with preparations for the next day's meals; my precious girls delighting in making fun crackers filled with an assortment of knickknacks which have been collected throughout the year; Roberto's demented family always insisted on store-bought crackers, as they were "proper—not rubbish."

The demented family was scheduled to arrive around six that evening—which generally means they'll arrive at about eight or nine, a situation that suited us perfectly. Around midday, I started to feel incredibly tense; Roberto jokingly offered me Rescue Remedy, and I prayed out loud for calm and strength (what could possibly go wrong between eight p.m. and nine a.m. the following morning?). There was an ominous knock at the door, and I cautiously peered through the window—Claude, Morrisa, Polly, and Tracy were at the door.

Their only greeting consisted of a demand: "What's for lunch?" The little girls would not even venture near my precious girls, who were ready to take them into the garden to play—Ashley desperate to be the "big" cousin for once. I responded, "We didn't plan on anything specific for lunch but I'll rustle up a few sandwiches quickly."

Morrisa, as usual, was positioned just behind Claude; she bent down and whispered her disdain directly into his ear. He then relayed her complaint: "We thought we'd get proper lunch after driving all this way—we are going out to eat."

They all promptly turned around, and Morrisa took delight in advising her girls, just loud enough for us to hear, "Don't worry, we'll go to Wimpy—then you can play on the jungle gym."

Ashley absolutely loved that restaurant's jungle gym, and she blurted out, "Please, may I go, Mom?"
Without missing a beat, Morrisa turned and, with a look of absolute triumph on her harsh face, snapped, "No, you may *not*—this is a family outing."

Ashley's little pixie face clearly showed her hurt; I swept her up and proceeded to run through the house and jump, fully clothed, into the pool to divert her broken heart. I was determined to protect my girls no matter what.

When they returned from their "family" outing, the girls were brandishing Happy Meal toys which they proceeded to play with. My precious girls were content to busy themselves with baking decorative kiekies with names for the Christmas tree. Around four o'clock, Claude announced they were going for a family walk around the block. My pixie didn't even ask to go, Alexis's arm protectively around her shoulder. When they returned, Polly and Tracy each proudly showed off the remnants of an ice cream, a packet of chips, and sweets. Neither of them offered a morsel to either of my girls. Eventually, these spiteful mini Morrisas relinquish their stronghold on their loot and join our girls, playing amicably in the back yard. Thankfully, the rest of the day passed without incident.

Around seven o'clock, Lucifer and Aradia arrived, laden with plastic containers, packets, and platters of edible food; Lucifer was on top form, slating our table decorations and lovingly decorated Christmas tree as "*pades* crap" (I assured my precious girls that he had already drunk enough for ten people that day). Lucifer always took great pride in his ability to belittle and insult me and my precious girls.

There was a house nearby where each year the family would erect hundreds of Christmas lights, decorations, and delightful paraphernalia; thousands of people would visit the home, and the owners would tell a Christmas story—every child's Christmas story coming to life in front of their very eyes. Ever since Alexis was born, Roberto and I would go through the home; in later years—for no reason I can make out—Lucifer and Aradia would come with us, much to my dismay.

In 2001, when Ashley was just seven and Alexis twelve, we made our pilgrimage to see the lights, for once just the four of us—joy of joys. Roberto's phone rang, and my blood ran cold. He babbled in Portuguese, as his eyes went small, and his furrow deepened. I awaited the onslaught, forcing myself to be positive. I had battled a weight problem since Ashley was born and was immensely proud that I could fit into a stylish pair of size 12 pants, teamed with a crisp white shirt and brown kitten heels. I felt beautiful, womanly—back straight, tummy tightly pulled in.

Aradia and Lucifer appeared to view the decorated house, and my heart sank. My precious girls' grip on my hands was blood stopping; Lucifer sidled up to us, cutting ahead of everyone in the queue, and in his loudest, cruellest voice, he proclaimed, "You go big and fat, Pippa, Roberto need buy a truck you fit."
Everyone had already turned to see who this loud, bombastic person was, and now I stood, totally ashamed, any sense of achievement destroyed. My humiliation was palpable. As always, Roberto pretended he didn't hear. In hindsight, I should have just said, "I can lose weight but you'll still be ugly." In that instance, at that time of my life, I just kept quiet, another knot in my already damaged soul.

Back to 2004: after dinner, we waited for midnight and the infamous present giving. Roberto and I had discussed this with our precious girls. We would not be opening presents on Christmas Eve; they would be opened in a delightful, happy, caring atmosphere on Christmas Day. As usual, Polly and Tracy were laden with discarded gifts, my precious girls receiving the standard R100-00 from Lucifer and Aradia.

My precious girls were excited at the idea of sleeping with their cousins in the lounge. We have had many sleepovers, with many girls forming a long line of bumps of all shapes and sizes, peppered with shrieks, giggles, and much to'ing and fro'ing to the kitchen and bathroom. That night, we fashioned a Christmas bed—but Polly and Tracy could not just sleep on a mattresses, they had to sleep in a small tent. But even though there was space, they would not let Ashley sleep in the tent with them. Alexis and I proceeded to make another tent over the chairs and table for my precious girls. All unkindness disguised, I came in to kiss my girls good night and noticed that every single window and fan light was firmly closed. In our home, whatever the season, whatever the weather, windows were usually opened, and at least all the fan lights were left on, not only for fresh air but for health reasons as well—germs breed far more quickly in a tightly sealed, warm room. We have always slept with the windows open; if they are closed we all get headaches.

In all innocence, I opened one of the fan lights. All mayhem broke out. Morrisa barged into the lounge, dragged both her girls out of the small tent, and marched them to Alexis's room to sleep, screaming the entire distance, "That woman is trying to kill my children, she just wants to make sure they get critically ill!"

Too shocked to move, I just lay down on the mattress in between my precious girls and prayed for daybreak. In her harsh, ear-piercing voice, Aradia reprimanded Roberto for having no control over his pades wife, calling me a terrible, useless mother, a disgrace to their wonderful, Christian family; with God's grace, my precious girls couldn't understand what she was saying. I translated for them but offer an innocuous, totally untrue version.

My precious girls and I woke up at dawn, extremely excited and looking forward to having our family in our home later that day for Christmas. I had a delightful CD of Christmas compilations and played it at full volume. My girls and I sang along at full volume. Roberto could not resist and joined in. All of a sudden, Claude came storming in from the garage, where he had been hiding in the car. He was furious that they had been disturbed. We pretended not to hear his furious ranting and raving. Let the games begin.

Our family started arriving to much laughter, friendly banter, and sneaking in of disguised presents; as usual, the ladies gravitated outside to enjoy a cup of tea, while the three brothers-in-law teamed up in the kitchen. Aradia started to berate Roberto.

David, Aleen's husband, firmly put her in her place, much to our delight. Oh, to have had the self-esteem to have done this right from the start. Perhaps then this demented family would not have been so cruel for so many years. "You marry at the level of your self-esteem," I once heard Mari Osmond say. Too true; when I was a teenager, I truly believed no one besides Roberto would ever be interested in me. So against my better judgment and intuition, I married him. A few weeks before the wedding, I was talking to my school friend in Italy and said I felt I was doing the wrong thing. She said I should just jump on a plane and hide out with her for a couple of months. I was sorely tempted. However, I didn't want to embarrass my mother and cause a scandal. I never thought of myself, just worried about what everyone else would say; that was what had been drummed into me my entire life. So for what seemed like a hundred endless years, I had taken intense emotional abuse, very rarely fighting back. Roberto also had incredibly low self-esteem, due to the command his parents had over him; he felt the need to dominate his family, doing it the only way he knew how, being intimidating and never entering into a discussion about anything he didn't feel fit to discuss.

Back to Christmas: a fun, laughter-filled day ensued, even though the demented DNA providers stayed for lunch (obviously eating only their own food; their loss). Our family totally enjoyed everything I had prepared. The presents were opened to much fun and general chaos. We all basked in the glow of love, joy, respect, and true family—shared DNA or not.

As the sun set, my precious girls and I watched God's magnificent spectacle, while knowing that He had heard our pleas to spend a pleasant day in our own home, with our family; it was truly memorable.

WINTER VISIT—2004

In July 2004, Roberto and I had been married for nineteen. We were expecting a visit from Roberto's parents, And even after all these years, I was still petrified of his family!

The air was crisp, the clouds hung low, and the early morning frost had burned my lush green lawn. Tensions ran high s we waited with trepidation for the in-laws to arrive. My precious girls, Alexis and Ashley, never called their father's parents grandparents; to be grandparents required a certain amount of love, respect, and joy shared between the parties.

Roberto, his parents, and his younger sister had emigrated from Portugal to South Africa in 1965. His younger brother, Claude, was born in South Africa in 1972 but still referred to himself as Portuguese. Aradia and Lucifer were fiercely patriotic—although their lives would have remained quite deprived if they had stayed in Portugal.

Most Portuguese immigrants in South Africa spoke minimal English. I found it totally disrespectful to the country that afforded you a much better life to not learn to speak English. There were countless European immigrants (Italians, Portuguese, Greeks) who came to this country and who did not speak English. That just proves their arrogance that they feel superior to South Africans.

These people had escaped their home countries to improve their standard of living, ensuring that their offspring actually had the opportunity of owning their own home one day, had access to top class medical facilities and education, and generally lived a life of luxury compared to what they had escaped from. Surely, then, they should consider themselves South Africans of Portuguese descent? Apparently not. Go to any gathering of Portuguese, and most will liberally criticise South Africa from beginning to end, but they all decline to move back to Portugal. Should they run off to Australia, they take citizenship and learning English within the prescribed five years for fear of being booted out! "Experience trumps assumption"; this has become my motto when this fact is disputed.

Many a time I have questioned how they can consider themselves Portuguese when they have lived, worked, and received medical attention in South Africa for forty-plus years. I firmly believe if they want to partake of the fruits of our magnificent country, then they should have the backbone to say they are South African of Portuguese descent!

Worse than not respecting our country enough to learn the language, these immigrants feel free to totally disrespect and detest South African women. The country was good enough for them to make a life here, but they absolutely cannot stand it if their sons marry a South African woman!

In January 1997, to save our sanity and our marriage, we moved to Standerton. On this Sunday morning in 2004, the only sound that cut through the frost and iciness was the excited chattering of my resident red-billed hoopoes, berating the cold, eager for their breakfast. We lived in a serene, friendly neighbourhood where all the neighbours respected each other's privacy.

The silence in the neighbourhood was shattered by a car's rude, vigorous honking. I took a deep breath and prepared for a tense, humourless day. My precious girls glanced at one another under their lashes in a silent pact to protect themselves and their mother.

Roberto opened the door and rushed out to the DNA providers' car. His parents trudged inside, laden with bowls, platters, and packets of food and beverages (as I am still incapable of making an edible meal—as was apparent to all, as my family was grossly undernourished and skeletal).

1983 I worked in a travel agency in Melville, then a hip and happening neighbourhood filled with artists, actors, and young couples. One Friday night Roberto and I would be alone at my mother's house. I decided to demonstrate my excellent culinary skills by cooking an entire meal from scratch. I went along to the local grocer and approached the fresh fish section, with a confidence that belied my lack of knowledge! Roberto loved fish and I asked for a red roman. "Would you like it like this?" the cheerful, round assistant enquired.

I looked horrified at her audacity. Really, what did she expect? Of course I was going to cook the entire fish? "Yes of course" I responded indignantly.

Her eye brows raised with tell tale experience, and with a knowing nod she packed the fish. After having slaved in the kitchen for hours, I presented Roberto with our dinner. As we tucked into the delectable Red Roman our mouths were filled with fish scales and innards. I was reduced to tears of laugher. At some later date Roberto enthusiastically regaled all present with the tale of my fish disaster, while I laughed and agreed fish was not my forte. Since then all and sundry have been well informed that being English I certainly will never be able to cook—anything, ever. That Monday during my lunch break, found me cap in hand at the fish counter, with the entire work force screaming with laughter. The assistant gleefully accepted my apology!

On that crisp July morning, the many packets, bowls, and a still warm pot are plonked down on my kitchen counter. The greetings were quick and terse. My precious girls and I consciously protected our chests from Lucifer's perversion; he always delighted in rubbing his chest against their yet undeveloped chests and my breasts, should we be unfortunate enough to be engulfed in an embrace by him. The sneer on his face was unmistakable whenever he accomplished this depraved act.

My every cell was on edge, waiting for the usual insults to the girls or about our home, weight, pimples, or general demeanour—covered by laughter and babbling in Portuguese between themselves. When no insults arise, my confidence grows and I innocently enquire, "Why don't you miss church today and spend time visiting with your granddaughters?"

Roberto's eyes grew as big as saucers. Only I would dare to suggest such evil, demonic behaviour. Aradia's voice became louder and brasher than usual: "No, I go shursh—you no go [sniff], you no dress [grunt],—uh, I go shursh."

I withered as three pairs of eyes condemned me—his parents, for being demonic, and Roberto, for my having the guts to actually make such a suggestion.

Let me elaborate: in Roberto's family, it was deemed proper Catholic behaviour to go to church twice a week, say several Hail Marys, have rosaries and statues of Mary all over the house, and yet be extremely judgmental, nasty, devious, and downright cruel whenever the urge arose. Christian behaviour included genuflecting, in utter submission and acceptance of all Catholic doctrine, when receiving the blessed sacrament of Holy Communion. But often, as they walked away from the altar, they would comment spitefully that Donna Lynda was wearing the same dress again or Donna Maria was getting really fat, and then nod at both of them with the kindest smile hiding their betrayal.

We all trooped to the door to see the DNA providers off to "shursh," already banished to hell for not attending church. The car is locked. We rushed around frantically, as Roberto searched in desperation for the keys. My girls and I stood in the kitchen, giggling. The nerve shattering ring of my cell phone shocked us into action. It was my precious, undiscriminating mother. "They've lost the car keys to go to shush," I confided with a delightful hint of laughter.

She replied playfully, "You little bugger, why did you hide them away?" I was innocent, I assured my mom, while containing my laughter so as to not seem guilty. Roberto then rushed in, looking extremely harassed and tense. "Where are the keys?" he demanded. "Come on, you can't hide them!"

I pleaded my innocence and rushed outside as the icy, silent air was filled with shrill screeches and chastising.

A blush rose from my belly to my head as I thought of my neighbours waking up to this cacophony of high-pitched shrieking admonishing everyone and everything for this extreme inconvenience. Lucifer stood on the pavement with his hands in his pockets" Benny Boek Wurm" glasses covered most of his pinched face, his nose red and vein covered from too many years of eager unabashed consumption of wine for breakfast, lunch and dinner. I hesitated, mid-lawn, not quite sure if I should approach the car or look inside. The purr of my neighbour's brand new Harley Davidson alerted me.

I looked up, and as my neighbour purred past, raising his hand in greeting, Lucifer made the most disgusting guttural, sucking sound and spat a huge glob of green slime towards the motorcycle, which landed perfectly on the back bumper of the sparkling Harley. Just then, I heard a shriek of achievement. The keys were found in the boot.

However, it was now too late for shursh!

FATHER'S DAY LUNCH–2007

In 2007, Ashley, my gorgeous, vivacious brunette, was in grade seven. She was friends with a really strange, very sullen, deathly pale, bottle blonde girl in her grade. This friendship seemed unlikely, and we often pondered their incompatible relationship. In retrospect, it was probably because she came from a broken home and her mother had many different boyfriends, most of whom were drunk. Another factor was that when she came home with Ashley, I was generally around to make lunch, act silly with them, and help with their dreaded homework.

Ashley was extremely petite, with a very sunny, happy personality. She laughed at absolutely everything, a coping mechanism my precious girls and I have developed to deal with the many very unpleasant situations we often found ourselves in. She had a gorgeous, sun-kissed face and dark hair.

The week after Father's Day, we were summoned to lunch at the DNA providers. Claude, Roberto's younger brother, and his family were going there on Father's Day. We could not imagine why we must visit Lucifer for Father's Day, as quite frankly he had never been very fatherly towards Roberto. However, as usual, taking the path of least resistance, we agreed to go.

Morrisa insisted that is was crucial for Polly and Tracey's, development so that they wouldn't become confused by the meaning of Fathers' Day that they could only have lunch with their very own father and his own father for fear of critically damaging their image of family hierarchy and relationships. Bizarre, yes! You ain't heard nothing yet! They therefore had Father's Day lunch with Lucifer and Aradia on Father's Day and we had to go the following week.

Roberto was ever the dutiful son. He was like a child who had been removed from his family and placed in foster care. He constantly yearned for his parents' acceptance and would never cross them, even to our detriment. This resulted in my extremely close relationship with our precious daughters. I was the backstop between Roberto's despicable behaviour with regards to his family and my precious daughters developing into well-adjusted, rational young ladies. Both Alexis and Ashley were fully aware that Roberto and his family's behaviour was totally unacceptable, demeaning, and archaic. I had drilled into them that my acceptance of their constant discrimination and humiliation was never to be repeated by them.

Alexis's long-term boyfriend knew only too well that any kind of ugliness from his family would result in her dropping him. Yes, all families have their disputes; it is quite normal. However, to be openly cruel for decades was truly evil personified.

This archaic behaviour had been demonstrated hundreds of times by Lucifer. Sitting at the dinner table for another enforced, dreaded Friday night dinner my nerves jangled as Lucifer commanded "Pass salt", his face pinched and very stern. The salt was in front of me. Exasperated at his extreme rudeness I raised my head and acted as though I haven't heard anything. He raised his voice and pulled his mouth into a thinner, more sadistic line. "Salt" he shouted. In all innocence I glanced at him as though he might be trying to get my attention. Infuriated he slammed his filthy fist onto the table and screams, "Pass salt". "Oh sorry do you need something" I responded calmly.

Roberto hastily grabbed the salt and literally ran around the table placing the salt in his father's grime encrusted hand. How could you humiliate yourself for such a rude, uncouth person I wondered? Then, quietly, in my sweetest little voice, I said "Please—(with great emphasis) may I have the salt"! He glared at me and held onto the salt as though his life depended on it.

All families have unspoken idiosyncrasies that no one discusses, but everyone knows they are present. Many are harmless, just verging on the embarrassing. However, I was privy to copious amounts of eavesdropping, as many stories were told in Portuguese in my blatant presence. For years, I never admitted that I understood their language and took in their constant gossip about their "friends" and their cruel ridicule of me and my precious girls. One day, I exploded, blurting out that what they had been saying was a lie! Aradia, Scorpio, Marcell, and Lucifer were furious, shocked, and even possibly scared that I'd repeat the many untrue, cruel stories that they now realised I'd been privy to. The gossiping then returned to whispers, behind closed doors.

With many innuendos flying around I gathered that Lucifer had a penchant for "chocolate". I couldn't fathom why Roberto looked at me as though I'd crawled out of cheese when I suggested we buy Lucifer chocolate to pacify him in some way! Initially I couldn't understand what the problem was as he always left the house for "chocolate" and why often quite crude jokes were made about "chocolate". Eventually Roberto confided that "chocolate" was in reference to black prostitutes. I was horrified. Not only was Lucifer a married man, a "devout" practicing Catholic, but he was one of the most racist Oizys males I have ever come across.

Archaic behaviour manifested itself on uncountable occasions. Lucifer would become roaring drunk. He would then proceed to leave the house to service his chosen piece of "chocolate" in any of the seedy, surrounding areas, where the local prostitutes plied their trade. This all took place during the height of apartheid in the 80's and early 90's, with all the Portuguese very openly professing to hate all blacks. He would then return home to beat his wife, once even putting a chopper in her head. His behaviour as the supposed head of the house hold, as many other Portuguese Oizys males, swept under the carpet.

Reluctantly, the week after Father's Day, we arrived at the prescribed restaurant; my mother had also been invited together with the strange friend Gabby. Lucifer and Aradia had chosen a fish restaurant, knowing full well that neither of my precious girls liked fish. During the humourless, strained greetings, I held my bag firmly in front of my chest to avoid Lucifer's disgusting, lecherous breast rub. As my girls developed and Roberto continued to avoid challenging his father's disgusting behaviour, these unwelcome greetings had become more physical.

I despised kissing random people, any people actually. I would at any given instant cover my precious girls with kisses while smothering them with hugs, but that's a different scenario altogether. What is the point if you don't really mean the intimacy that a shared hello kiss implies? True to Portuguese duplicity you kiss everyone you come into contact with on both cheeks. This is done if you despise them or not. Heaven help me on the occasions that I have declined this greeting. I may as well have been hung, drawn and quartered.

Alexis and I gestured to one another in utter confusion when Gabby was greeted with the standard Portuguese kiss while Ashley was left standing on the outskirts, not knowing what to do. Roberto got furious should one of my precious girls not comply and greet his DNA providers in the traditional way. Ashley was left giggling in embarrassment for herself and Gabby who was totally bewildered!

We endured an unpleasant lunch, with Roberto trying to divide his attention between us and Lucifer and Aradia. Their English was totally forgotten for today. My precious mother, as always, made small talk and tried to lighten the atmosphere. My precious girls and I escaped into our own little worlds, blocking off the obvious rejection and contempt shot at us by Lucifer and Aradia.

With the eternal, tense lunch over, we made our way to the car to hand over another unwelcomed Father's Day gift to Lucifer. Every time my precious girls would give him a gift, he would totally insult them by verbalising his distaste for their present. We normally gave him a shirt from Woolworths; he would probably prefer a bottle (or six) of alcohol, which I firmly refused to consider. Scorpio and Marcell always indulged his taste for alcohol at every special event, thereby making them the gift-giving kings of the family.

While Alexis and Ashley went through the ritual of giving Lucifer his unappreciated gift, Aradia was rummaging in her huge handbag. I watched as Aradia proceeded to hand an envelope to Alexis and then to Gabby, who looked as though she was about to throw up. Ashley stood to the side, unable to contain her great confusion!

Her hazel eyes had grown wide with hurt, bigger than those of the platters the fish was served on, her face redder than the finest Valentine's rose. For once, Roberto openly showed his disgust and disappointment. "Gu bi Aashli" ("Good-bye Ashley"), Aradia said, as she leaned into Gabby to accept the required double kiss. Gabby was absolutely motionless, her ashen face a totally blank canvas, her eyes wide with shock.

Neither of the DNA providers noticed that anything was amiss and strutted off, mumbling in Portuguese to one another. Gaby, more bewildered than ever, tried to hide her obvious embarrassment, while holding out the envelope to Ashley. Gabby later confided that kissing these strange people made her feel totally sick to her stomach, and she felt terribly guilty that her friend's Grand parents had obviously confused them.

On the way home, we all joked about how "you can choose your friends but you can't choose your relatives." That fateful day, Aradia and Lucifer had put the final nail in their coffin as far as Ashley was concerned. Since that day, cementing the fact that she has never referred to them as her grandparents in any form again. She openly states that she has a "Dassie," and her beloved Papa passed away when she was nearly two. No reference is ever made of Roberto's DNA providers as grandparents.

KETIWE'S FIRST MEETING WITH
ROBERTO'S DNA PROVIDERS—2007

Alexis matriculated in 2006 with exceptional results. Studying always came easily to my precious gift from God. Her inquisitive mind always made me proud, sometimes with hilarious consequences. When she was about seven, she often heard me call Roberto a wanker; after one such incident, Alexis asked what that word meant. I replied that it was not something she had to know about at this stage of her life. A while later, in her sweet, innocent voice, she asked, "Mom, what's masturbating?" Shocked, I replied, "It's not something you need to know about now." Five minutes later, she returned, with her eyes as big as saucers; visibly unhappy, she blurted out, "Mom, does my dad really do that?" Apparently, Alexis had looked up each word in the dictionary to satisfy her curiosity when I wouldn't.

In December of 2006, while on holiday to Cape Town, we received her excellent results and were all ecstatic. Since birth, Alexis has been the kindest, most generous, loving soul. Wherever she is, people naturally gravitate to her, often pouring out their heartache to her and asking her counsel. She finds this exhausting, as she takes everyone's problems onto herself and really wants to help them. She feels their pain and wishes she could sort everything out. It has taken many long hours of discussion for me to convince her to avoid being swamped. No surprise, then, that she was Head of Learner Affairs.

After receiving her results, Alexis came to me early one morning, looking very distressed. She really didn't want to go away to study, as she felt a deep need to stay and work at the local hospice day care facility that cared for HIV-infected and affected preschoolers. Alexis wanted to give something back to our community. Ashley was ecstatic, as she did not want her sister leaving her. I've always firmly believed that God has his hand on all such decisions, and what a plan he had in store for us!

Alexis would go off to the hospice creche every morning and return with tales of cute kids, snotty noses (that gave her the creeps), and lots of hugs. In February, a new little girl was brought in who was gravely ill. Ketiwe's mommy had died in a car accident, and her father had abandoned her at the hospital while she was critically ill. No other family member ever tried to find her.

There was an instant, deep connection between Alexis and Ketiwe. As time passed, we often collected Ketiwe from the in-patient unit and brought her to our home to spend Saturdays with us; we would spoil her rotten and shower her with love and attention. She didn't speak a word of English, only her mother tongue, Tswana.

She now only speaks English and was very proud to announce she had learnt some Tswana at school the other day (late 2010): "oh really let me hear" I asked bemused. "Haw whena" (colloquial slang for hey you), she announced with great pride!

No matter what, Ketiwe made us smile every day. We fondly referred to her as our little blessing. She would get extremely excited when we arrived to collect her, and then she'd sob when we would take her back.

In July of 2007, Alexis went off to college in Krugersdorp. Ashley and I were devastated at the prospect of only seeing her every two weeks.

Alexis, Ashley, and I are inordinately close due to the relentless, ruthless discrimination, humiliation, and constant tension from Roberto's DNA providers.

Why have I stayed? I did try to leave at the end of 1990 but I had absolutely no support from anyone. My mom firmly advised me "People in our family don't get divorced". Me being totally insecure, convinced that should I leave I would never have another relationship as I was totally undesirable and really lucky that Roberto had taken pity on me and married me! My entire life I had taken the path of least resistance. Having always lived in an atmosphere of constant altercations, jostling for attention, avoiding confrontation at all costs. I constantly prayed that with time and maturity, things would get better. Had we not moved to Standerton in 1997, I am sure Roberto and I would have divorced. The all consuming hatred and discrimination still raged on, but thankfully from afar. We only had to deal with occasional visits.

As the girls became older, the three of us have literally ganged up on Roberto to make him actually look at how he behaved towards us after any contact with his DNA providers. He has eventually realised that his behaviour was absolutely unfathomable and truly uncalled for.

It is as if his mother controlled his every emotion from afar. Each time she phoned an unexplained incident occurred. During December of 2009 we were on holiday in Umdloti. There were hundreds of eager monkeys that took every opportunity to enter the apartment we had rented and grabbed what—ever they could. Roberto was fastidious about making sure all the doors and windows were definitely securely locked against their desperate desired invasion.

Early one morning Aradia started phoning. Thankfully I had his phone and kept silencing the relentless calls. With every fibre of my being I wished that she would just leave us in peace. No such luck, she phoned five times and eventually Roberto answered. Her command was very clear. Roberto MUST phone some pension person and confirm an appointment. A task he undertook immediately. The baffled pension man became irritated as he had already confirmed the appointment and spoke a good deal of Portuguese.
The unease in my belly rendered me silent as previous such incidents had always resulted in some form of discord and or trouble. I prayed that my family would be safe.

Off we went and had a fun sun filled family day. I banished an uneasy feeling, determined that nothing would upset these few stolen days. The day ws delightful, the beach warm, the surf inviting. We arrived home happy, relaxed and looking forward to seeing our niece Jessica and her fiancé Jordan.

I opened the front door. Irritated I noticed a piece of bread on the floor near the bedroom door and instantly assumed that Ketiwe had dropped it. Always aware that I must avoid confrontation at all costs, Roberto would be furious at such a deed, I hastily stepped into the apartment, to dispose of the offending piece of bread before Roberto noticed, and chaos greeted me. Every cupboard in the kitchen was open, discarded food and peels were strewn all over the lounge, dining room and kitchen. The far sliding door was wide open. A defiant male monkey starred me directly in the eyes, with a look of total triumph and accomplishment covering his nasty little face.

Later, Jordan, as big as he is, battled to open the unlocked sliding door. Was this a coincidence or an evil deed summons from afar? I couldn't help but mention that Aradia had phoned for nonsense that morning! I was always aware of her dark side and that she had unashamedly dabbled in Witch Craft.

Often now Roberto will arrive home and we'll all hide our heads pretending to protect ourselves. We do this when his eyes are small and line in the middle of his forehead a deep furrow of frustration and uncertainty. This is a sure sign that he has spoken to one of his DNA providers, normally Aradia. We then wait for Roberto to unleash his frustration brought on by some obscure ranting and or accusations heaped on him by Aradia. With God's grace and our collective strength these out bursts have become few and far between and when they do occur they are much less severe. Roberto eventually realised that Aradia manipulated him unashamedly.

In October 2007, the hospice CEO asked our family to look after Ketiwe for the entire month of December. We agreed instantly, and on December ninth, I collected Ketiwe for an extended stay. What an extended stay it turned out to be!

We were supposed to take Ketiwe back to the Hospice in patient unit at the end of January 2008 and we just could not, knowing for sure that she would just become another statistic in an already over burdened system. Also knowing for sure that the aids virus would take over her little body and she would surely die.

Ashley, Alexis and I asked God for a tangible sign should it be the right thing for our family to accept Ketiwe into our family. John three verse sixteen is a very profound verse in the bible—"For God so loved the world that He gave His only begotten son, who so ever believes in him should not perish but have everlasting life."—and so we sat on my bed together and asked God to show us this piece of scripture. The next Sunday Joyce Meyers preached on John three verse sixteen and that week I received a valentines email from a girl friend about John three sixteen! Needless to say our little blessing became our daughter and sister!

The CEO of Hospice was delighted with our decision but cautioned us that Kitiwe would more than likely not see then end of the year due to her high viral load and cd4 count.

Ketiwe turned eight this November (2012) and the HIV virus is barely detectable!

During the December of 2007,we had great fun dressing her, playing games, and trying to figure out what she was saying at any given time. She had just turned three and was recovering from a severe case of TB. She was not infectious but had to take copious amounts of medication. She was also HIV+.

We delighted in her absolute joy at the simplest of things. She relished lying flat on her tummy in the shower, drinking the water from the shower floor while chanting happily, "Warm *pula* [rain]." She would make her index finger absolutely straight and lick countless fingers of tomato sauce, giggling at every lick. She would also snuggle up on our laps and just stare into our eyes with absolute trust and love. She was the most adorable little thing we had ever encountered. Without any prompting, she began calling me "Mama" and wanted me to be in her line of vision at all times. I couldn't help hugging, kissing, and holding her for a huge part of the day. Today, after being just a little brown body with no personality or hope when she arrived with us, she has morphed into a unique combination of Alexis's gentle, kind, and generous spirit and Ashley's straight-talking, no-nonsense attitude.

On Christmas Eve in 2007, we met Roberto's parents for lunch at the local shopping centre. With my mom and Ketiwe in tow, we were all extremely tense, as at the best of times Roberto's parents would discriminate against us. With us now having an African child, we couldn't imagine what the reaction would be.
Terse greetings ensued on our arrival, our handbags firmly in place so that my precious girls and I could avoid the perverted breast rub at all costs.

We took our seats, but before we even had menus Aradia's brash, harsh, ear-piercing voice barked, "This *preta* (black girl), she have death sickness?" My blood ran cold. All of us, including Roberto, pretended we didn't hear this absurd question. Louder now, while glaring directly at me, she repeated. This *preta* she have death sickness?"

My mothers' jaw actually dropped and her eyes widened. Roberto shifted uncomfortably in his seat and said slowly in English, "What's a death sickness, senora?".
Sniffing, snorting, and shaking her head, she replied—"You know all *pretas* have a death sickness. Too much no pure. She has?"
I grew exasperated and stated firmly, "No. As far as I know there is no such thing as a death sickness. So no this delightful little girl can't have it."

Thinking the situation was averted, Roberto visibly relaxed and was about to start chatting about the menu, but then the gurgling and clearing of spit from Lucifer's throat cracked the uncomfortable silence. He looked at me and said, "So you Pipa, you get *preta* AIDS to come live with you and kill you all?" He cackled at his own great sense of humour. "Well, actually it was Alexis," I explained. "And no, she doesn't have AIDS. She is HIV+, which is vastly different. If we should all die, it will surely be from your unkindness!" I whispered with a sarcastic smile plastered on my snow white angry face. And the without even taking a breath, I added, "I'll have the surf and turf." After ordering, I bent to kiss our little blessing directly on her sticky lips.

In February of 2009 Ketiwe started at the local Catholic pre-school. After I had received information that swimming lessons were to be presented by a staunch Catholic Portuguese local woman, I duly completed the application, adding that Ketiwe was HIV+ should there be any mishap. We were all delighted as Ketiwe loved swimming and the lessons would bring a degree of safety to our pool. That evening I received a very disturbing telephone call. It was the swimming teacher "Unfortunately Ketiwe would not be accepted for the swimming lessons". "Why" I enquired. I was totally shocked. "Well what if she was to wee in the pool? The entire swimming school would get AIDS and then I will be sued", she shouted at me. This ignorance was too great to fathom and no amount of explaining that thousands of HIV+ people use public pools and the sea everyday with no effect on anyone around them would change her mind.

It took an in depth workshop from Hospice to convince the swimming instructor that she and her swimming school were safe from imminent disaster. No amount of reasoning could make her believe that there are hundreds of white, fit, fat and pushing forty males and females who are HIV+. She firmly believed it was only the" impure prêts" (blacks) and "those disgusting men" who could pass on the disease! Lord have mercy, Christ have mercy, Lord grant us peace.

On a sweltering day in November of 2011, while shopping in our local Hyper we bumped into a well known, well established Portuguese couple. We chatted amicably about children, grand children and boyfriends. "So how's your one with cancer?" the lady enquired. Confused I explained that I didn't understand. "You know the one you adopted ". Thinking she had the wrong end of the stick I proceeded to correct the misunderstanding. "Oh, she doesn't have cancer she's HIV+". With utter sincerity she responded' "so that's the same thing, especially in the prêts!" I considered laughing out loud but instead I was filled with absolute shock and dismay. She was 100% certain that cancer, being HIV+ and having full blown AIDS are one and the same thing. I tried to explain that being HIV+ is a virus which attacks the immune system, and is not a growth that can possibly be removed. All my intricate medical explanations were to no avail. She was adamant that "Prêts" have this cancer and it was all their own fault and totally disgusting. The shocking comment that made my stomach turn and my heart ache was, "No offence to you but really you must know that these prêts are just too much. They just can't help themselves! But never mind its wiping them out!" she visibly shuddered. At this stage of the conversation I could have sobbed with utter frustration, anger and shame. I have failed to mention that firstly she always waxes lyrical about reading every glossy magazine available and drinking in their current information and secondly that she was a devout, church going Catholic! The last I checked the Bishop of the local Roman Catholic Diocese is "a prêt". Christ have mercy, Lord have mercy, God grant us peace.

During the uncomfortable, confrontational Christmas lunch the air in the Portuguese restaurant was thick with discord and unspoken aggression. During the meal, as always, the conversation was divided into two groups: the pades chatting, laughing, and generally just enjoying one another's company at one end of the table, and the DNA providers at the other end, discussing only ugliness and bad events about everything and everyone in their cruel world. At some stage during the meal, I could feel Roberto's entire demeanour transform into a very uncomfortable, shocked being who wished he could escape to the farthest planet. Glancing over at him, I noticed that his complexion was a light shade of green and then visibly red. He didn't finish his calamari, a delectable dish he usually relished. This was extremely strange and disconcerting.

When lunch was over, I cornered Roberto outside the restaurant. He said he felt physically ill and was almost hyperventilating; visibly shocked, he confided that he had had a shocking encounter with Aradia, who had quite openly explained to him, in explicit detail, that she had a severe vaginal infection. She described the colour, odour, and consistency of the disturbing, disgusting discharge, which was also extremely itchy, hence her constant wiggling during lunch. Aradia was sure her husband had passed the disgusting infection on to her.

Roberto then suffered a bout of excruciating heartburn and vomited all over the pavement. The grey pallor did not leave his stricken face until the next day. He was totally horrified by the entire incident. I was not sure if he was more distressed by Aradia explaining the infection to him or by this confirmation that Lucifer and Aradia actually have sex. For his entire life, Aradia had ranted and raved about purity so intensely that I was sure in his heart of hearts, Roberto imagined that he was immaculately conceived! The very notion of Lucifer and Aradia actually copulating had sickened him to his very core.

EVIL VISSION—2009

On a freezing cold night in April of 2009, the eerie stillness of midnight was interrupted by an unwelcome knot in my stomach. The night sky was illuminated by the perfectly round full moon—which was symbolic of the height of power, the peak of clarity, the fullness and obtainment of any evil desire. The full moon is seen as a helpful time in all types of magic and where power is needed most. This is a powerful time where energy is in abundance. Magical rites are amplified as energy is in its zenith.

I was not quite awake nor quite asleep, a state I've come to dread. I had curled further into the foetal position, seeking protection from the vision I knew was about to present itself.

For years, I have known that I was a "highly sensitive and intuitive person" (HSP). Most people think I speak rubbish or believe I think I'm better than anyone else. But studies have shown that such people take in a lot, all the subtleties that others miss. When most people walk into a room, they notice the furniture and the people; that's about all. The HSP will be instantly aware, whether they wish to or not, of the mood, the friendships and enmities, the freshness or staleness of the air, even the personality of the person who arranged the flowers. HSPs instantly know who can be trusted and who cannot, an experience I was often familiar with.

Since I can remember, I have had feelings about people, places, and events. I'd meet someone and instantly feel uncomfortable, sometimes,

90

actually scared. My mother and siblings often said I was rude and should just keep quiet.

I knew instinctively who to trust and who to steer clear of, once again being labelled anti-social. I had the uncanny ability to sense exactly what a person was like, even by just speaking to them on the phone; I could sense immediately if they drank too much, were jealous, were dishonest, or were just general troublemakers. I learnt not to verbalise my feeling to anyone but my precious girls, as people tended to get extremely angry should I blurt out, "Your son is on drugs" (I was called "a self-absorbed jealous bitch" for that faux pas, but not long after that, the person's son landed in rehab; no apology was forthcoming).

I came to trust the feelings of unease that presented themselves at any given moment.

On one such occasion in 1998 I was too scared to tell Roberto that we really shouldn't go to Lucifer's birthday lunch, we had to drive 200 km's one way, as I knew he would just refuse to accept my inner voice as real and would accuse me of not wanting to go. How very true. To be spared the agony of being in the same city, let alone around the same table as those evil, destructive beings, would have been too generous of an act from Roberto. Off we went. We all struggled though lunch. The heavy atmosphere ensured indigestion for days! The feeling of imminent danger made my every nerve tense. Eventually with the lunch over we left. Totally out of my control my senses were on high alert. I kept shivering involuntarily. I tried in vain to just relax and be calm. I repeated a mantra my maternal granny used frequently—"peace, peace, peace be still". I felt the need to sit on the back seat with my precious girls. This totally rankled Roberto. He wasn't a taxi. Much to his annoyance I didn't give in. My only thought was that I needed to protect my precious girls. Then for no apparent reason the van went totally out of control and we slid helplessly across a busy intersection and crashed into the pavement. Instinctively I pushed both my precious girls heads down into my lap. Had I not done that Ashley would of hit her head on the window and who knows what injury she would of sustained. The uncontrollable vehicle stopped and a sense of deep calm washed over me. Thank God no one was injured.

In April of 1980 when I met Aradia formally for the first time after Roberto had taken me to see *Kramer versus Kramer.* Before I actually saw her the hairs on the back of my neck stood up and an icy cold shiver travelled from the tips of my toes to the top of my head and almost stopped my heart on its journey. I didn't understand this feeling at all. It just engulfed me as she walked towards us. Just as alarming was when I met, Scorpio for the first time. Fear gripped my heart that made me what to throw up. There was cruel, unadulterated evil personified in both of them. On meeting Lucifer the sense of perversion and a hunger to dominate all in his wake made me shy away from his traditional Portuguese greeting of a kiss on each cheek. A greeting my precious girls and I would come to hate as he always made sure he would rub his chest against our breasts unless we firmly place a handbag between us. This perverse action was even carried out on my dear mother, much to her horror and shock.

New year's eve of 2001 was fun and care free. We had spent the evening at the community centre and my precious girls and I had a lot of fun. For the first time in the longest time I danced with them and just had fun totally ignoring Roberto's DNA providers who looked on with absolute scorn. My behaviour confirmed, for them, in no uncertain terms, that I was a *pades puta!*

I have tried a million times to try and fathom why they insisted on spending nearly every New Years Eve with us in Standerton for about seven years after we moved here. To no avail. They were clearly very unhappy being here, but each year they would return. When I questioned Roberto he got decidedly angry. In my heart I think they did it just to be difficult as each year inevitably there was a huge issue about something! Since I have known them they have thrived on adversity and unhappiness.

After our fun evening at the community centre we returned home at about twelve thirty and I made coffee for us. There was added excitement in the air for Alexis as she had just finished primary school and the new year in which she was to start high school had just dawned. There was a knock on the door; it was Darren, her school friend who was moving on to the same high school. She went outside and chatted with him for a time while I was in the back lounge. When she came back in, I blurted out, "Why did Darren come and ask you for money for cigarettes?" As soon as this proclamation was out, I wanted to take it back, but by looking at the absolute shock and horror that crossed Alexis's face, I knew in no uncertain terms that I was absolutely correct. How did I know that? I have no idea. I just knew!

2009 was a life-changing year for us in more ways than one—changes that you will read about later.

Alexis, Ashley, and Jan went to visit Jessica and Jordan in Durban in December. They were returning on the fourteenth, and on the fifteenth Alexis had an appointment with the endocrinologist for some test results. For the entire day, I was worse than a cat on a hot tin roof. My nerves were shredded, and I phoned the girls a hundred times during their return journey. After they arrived home safely, I decided that my extreme unease was due to the anguish regarding the outcome of the blood tests. For the entire day, every time I walked past my home office, I shivered. Sleep came slowly to me, and when I did dose off it was fitfully.

Around two o'clock, I woke up feeling terrified and in desperate need of the bathroom. As I walked past our bedroom door to our en suite bathroom, I felt the most ominous presence and had the inexplicable urge to just get out of the house. As I returned to the bedroom, I heard the distinctive sound of the office window closing as the latch slid back into place. My heart froze and I woke Roberto. We checked my office and I noticed that my laptop was gone. We had been robbed! The police came, they took our statements, and Roberto returned to bed. I was still extremely distressed and paced through my home relentlessly. Around three o'clock, a car pulled into my driveway and three men approached my office once more! I yanked open the front door and screamed, "In the name of God go away! Bugger off! I knew you were coming back!" In the moonlight, I could see the utter shock on their faces as they turned and disappeared into the night. On cue, a sense of calm engulfed me. I was safe. The danger had passed.

When we told this to the investigating officer, he said that homeowners often hear a sound, go and check, think they are crazy, and take a sleeping tablet and go back to sleep. The thieves then return about an hour later to take the rest of the loot they identified earlier!

The midnight April air was freezing, my being taunt with fear and unease. Then a vision presented itself to me. This vision was so real I could feel every cruel, evil aspect of it. I was in the room next to the kitchen in Roberto's DNA providers' house. It had been his bedroom growing up. A putrid odour engulfed the house, worse than normal. There had never been any love, happiness, or kindness between these four walls. Only evil: manifested in a stale, putrid odour of discord.

In my terrified half-asleep, half-awake state, a pungent smell that burned my nose emanated from the cupboard. I yanked open the cupboard door and saw three dolls; to my shock, they bore an uncanny resemblance to my precious girls and myself. There were pins in the stick-like figures. I turned to see Aradia glaring at me, insane with rage that I had discovered the depth of her demonic conjuring. She gave a sadistic grin and calmly said, with utter hatred, "I make you blood bad. You suffer."

Horrified and fearing for my precious girls' safety, I called out, "No. I turn this onto your blood now; you aren't going to carry on hurting me and my precious girls," and then I fled.

I was shocked to my core at the depths to which she would sink to destroy us—all because her son didn't marry a Portuguese girl. It did not matter that my girls were leaders, always polite, and achieved exceptionally well at school. Nothing mattered unless you were Portuguese.

Over the years I have come to learn that anything is excusable and acceptable if you are "Portuguese".

Morissa had, on more than one occasion, shouted at Aradia "fuck off you bitch". Natasha, at the ripe old age of 6 spat out scornfully "shud up (shut-up) and just bloody do what I say. You are stupid anyway". Polly, aged 4 with utter disdain on several occasions was heard to say "why the hell should I listen to you. You old fucking bag". As long as you are Portuguese that is totally acceptable behaviour. God help us if anyone of us had gone anywhere near those insults.

For the longest time people in general would relate stories of how friendly and inviting the Portuguese community was. How one was always offered a meal and invited over. However if one was in that inner circle there are countless horrendous accounts of husbands beating their wives and children after these "wonderful" visits as the soup was a bit cold, or the wife was too friendly to one of the men. Or one of the men was too friendly to the wife, even if she ignored him it would still be her fault. My associate was privy to this shocking violent behaviour, often bathing bruises and calming distraught bruised children. The "outside" world oblivious to this disgusting violent behaviour. As always the doctor paid a large cash sum ensuring his continued silence.

When I questioned Roberto about this despicable behaviour his explanation was that the Portuguese father's had always been violent, having very short fuses, loosing their tempers at the drop of a hat. That the new generation were just following their father's example. Very few chose to break the cycle of abuse and womanising.

Eventually I woke fully on this freezing April witching hour—it was freezing cold but I was drenched in sweat. I woke up, struggling to breathe, and wondered what this meant for us as a family. I had come to trust these visions. I prayed fervently; for days after this terrifying vision, I didn't sleep. I didn't mention this most disturbing dream to anyone.

The next month came, when we were to celebrate my forty-fifth birthday. You will read about that in the next chapter.

ROBERTO'S ILLNESS—MAY 2009

Wednesday, 14 May 2009, dawned bright and sunny; it was my forty-fifth birthday; I had been with Roberto for twenty-nine long years. I woke up to a delightful birthday text message from my precious gift from God, Alexis, who was working in Johannesburg. I missed her terribly when she was gone! Next, my precious little pixie, Ashley, bounded into my room with our little blessing, Ketiwe. They both jumped into my bed, covering me with kisses. Soon, Roberto left to take Ashley to school and then returned to run the bath. As part of our morning ritual, we would bathe together as we chatted amicably.

Our lives were about to change irrecoverably.

Suddenly, in the middle of our conversation, Roberto started moaning and gripping his side. He looked deathly pale and began hyperventilating. I jumped out of the bath, my mind on high alert. Hundreds of random thoughts clouded all logic: How could I get underpants on him? He wouldn't want to be collected by an ambulance stark naked (we've discussed this many times). How could I prevent him from drowning in the bath? (In my great distress, I don't realise that I could just pull out the plug.) In hindsight, it can be quite shocking to relive one's reactions in a crisis. I totally panicked and lost all rational thoughts. With great effort, I got Roberto out the bath, dressed him, and drove him to the doctor's office. We were sent straight to the local private hospital.

As Roberto was being admitted, my mom called, all cheery and excited, to ask where we were, as she'd arrived as a surprise for my birthday. In immense distress, I sobbed as I told her we were at the hospital. All day, my stress was perpetuated, as my family and friends phoned to wish me happy birthday. I very seldom disclosed personal problems to anyone until I am sure of the outcome, but each time I received a phone call, I explained this very distressing situation.

The day was a blur of tests, doctors, specialists, and phone calls; Alexis returned home, and through this entire process, Roberto was in excruciating pain and refused to utter a word. He just lay motionless in the stark white hospital bed, arching his back each time he was wracked with pain.
Roberto's refusal to speak was extremely disconcerting and distressing. Even when the girls went to see him, he didn't react at all. He would not even speak to the nurses and doctors. This behaviour made us all fear the worst, as normally Roberto had a lot to say about everything, and no matter what the situation, he could always find something to complain about.

By the end of visiting hours, my precious girls and I were exhausted, emotionally drained, and fearful. Roberto still hadn't uttered a word. We went home, and the girls and I tried to calm one another and prayed that the next day we'd get some answers. Around nine o'clock, Roberto's phone rang. It was Aradia. I answered his phone, and before I could begin to explain about his condition, Aradia made it quite clear that she was most annoyed that I dared answer the phone. After some hesitation, I explained that Roberto was in hospital, critically ill, with no diagnosis. In her harsh guttural voice, she started berating me. "Why you no hospital?" she shouted.

A random stupid thought crossed my mind; quite frankly, I was fed up that after being in this country for over forty years, she still spoke such broken English; I felt like answering, "Because the last time I checked I was a person, not a building." Regretfully, I have to audibly swallow the retort.
"Go hospital now, give to Roberto *olio* [oil]!" she demanded.
In shock, I responded quietly, "Sorry, I don't understand."
Her voice grew harsher and louder: "You quiet, hear now: give Roberto half bottle *azeite* [olive oil]. Now. You go. You listen."

This instruction was totally ridiculous. "Roberto is actually critically ill, and at the best of times one can't drink half a bottle of olive oil," I explained with much restraint. I was totally floored and couldn't decide if I should laugh or cry. My precious girls, who could hear the exchange, were hysterical, almost rolling on the floor.

The tempo of her harsh, ear-piercing voice increased: "You go give azeite now I tell you, he toilet all fix."
My patience up, I raised my voice and firmly stated, "No, absolutely no olive oil; bowel movements don't cure all ailments."
I heard a click and the line went dead. My girls and I stared at one another and thanked our lucky stars that she was 200 kilometres away.

In shock, we stood in the kitchen, trying to fathom the logic of olive oil curing all ailments. Suddenly, we were jarred out of our introspection as Roberto's phone rang once more. It was Claude. With no greeting, he demanded, "Where is my brother? Why aren't you at the hospital?"

Hesitantly, I began to answer but he interrupted before I could continue.
"What kind of person are you to be at home?"
I tried to speak again: "I have . . ." but again the rest of my explanation was cut off.
"Why don't you do as my mother says? What's wrong with you?"
Once again, I tried in vain to explain the gravity of the situation; I started, "But Roberto . . ." The rest of my sentence was cut off while it swirled silently in my head: "is really ill and I can't leave my girls alone at home and there is absolutely nothing I can do at the hospital right now." However, none of these thoughts were verbalised. Claude's voice pounded my buzzing head, his voice harsh and accusatory: "You *must* listen to my mother and give Roberto the *azeite.*"
In utter shock and hurt, I shouted, "Because he is in the best hospital in the province and I have three daughters and a business to look after. There's no diagnosis; he can't be given *azeite.*" For the next five minutes, I was berated for being rude, uncaring, and stupid. The phone was on speakerphone, and my girls were flabbergasted that I was being spoken to in this manner.
This lecture and verbal lambasting was heaped upon my terrified being by a "boy" 10 years my junior who used to be sweet and extremely kind.

The cool uncle. The brother-in-law everyone wished for. The uncle who loved his nieces,(and me for that matter) and took them for joy rides in his beetle without a roof, who played ball with them and was always be ready for a laugh. The delightful, calm, friendly young man who used call me up at work demanding his favourite dish for dinner. I always obliged happily. My life line that somewhere within Roberto's DNA providers there was a shred of humanity.

I still can't help recalling with great delight an incident that occurred when Alexis was about 5. We were living in Krugersdorp and often all the cousins played at our home. Kevin (7) and Shaun (10) were getting up to no good boy nonsense as usual when I heard a louder than normal commotion. On investigating Claude had popped in for a quick cup of tea and to see the kids, as he often did. The boys had very kindly sold him a bottle of "home-made juice"! I smelt a rat! Their utterly mischievous expressions of intense anticipation belied their innocence. In the nick of time I grabbed the "juice" only to discover that it was the boys pee! Chaos ensued as Claude chased them around bent on revenge, pale at the thought of almost sipping their urine. However he saw the funny side and enjoyed a good laugh about it many times thereafter. Sadly years later, when he related this story to Morrissa she instantly turned it into a shocking tale of perverted behaviour by unruly disgusting *pades* hooligans. How very sad!

I'm jolted back to my immense worry and the electrified atmosphere in my kitchen, once again realising that Claude had been kind, loving and gentle UNTIL 1996 when he became involved with a Portuguese tyrant—Morrissa, who cut off his balls and turned him into her self controlled puppet! Eventually, I just agreed to all my many short-comings and hung up. I then sat on the floor and sobbed with every ounce of my shattered soul.

The long suppressed memories of Claude being the little brother I never had, my friend, pierce my heart. Alexis quietly recalled how he used to be so kind and loving to us all—Alexis and Ashley's cousins included. Then along came Morrissa. She was horrified that his brother had married a *pades* and from day one made her displeasure very plain. In her limited vision the "pure" Portuguese linage had been tainted. I have pondered a million times, if the Portuguese are so very obsessed with keeping their race "pure", why then did any of them ever leave Portugal for greener pastures if all things Portuguese are so exceptional?

Eventually, my precious girls and I curled up in my bed and got some sleep, however fitful. Thursday and Friday passed in a blur of invasive, extremely painful tests, along with numerous abusive (and even more invasive) phone calls from Aradia and Claude. These calls insisted on treating Roberto with azeite, spiritual healers, and homeopaths. I dreaded answering any phone. My nerves were in shreds. I was physically and emotionally exhausted, perpetuated by the fact that there was still no diagnosis.

Roberto still hadn't uttered a single word since we left the house Wednesday morning. He just lay in the bed, wincing periodically with his eyes closed. This behaviour was totally soul destroying and made the entire episode extremely scary for my precious girls. The phone next to his hospital bed rang incessantly, always Claude, Aradia, or Lucifer, demanding to speak to Roberto, who just shook his head and turned away. They refused to believe he didn't want to speak on the phone. Eventually, we disconnected it.

The doctor phoned—he suspected terminal cancer. My precious girls and I gathered together on my bed and called our dearest friends in Cape Town, who were kind and supportive. My sisters phoned constantly, with gentle words of support and loving messages from my cousins, aunts, and their own extended families. My mother, being the bushveld telegraph, had every extended family member and church prayer group in action. She handled phone calls, the door, and even my clients.

The calls from Roberto's DNA providers were relentless, with more abusive phone calls accusing us of lying about not knowing the diagnosis. I was accused of not sharing information from the doctors; they even continued to demand we force-feed him *azeite*. We were totally numb.

Saturday morning dawned cold and very windy; there was a distinct undertone of evil and unrest lurking in the depths of my being—a sure sign that something horrifying was about to transpire. My nerves were in shreds, as I have learnt to trust these feelings. They were never wrong. The doctor had ordered an MRI, and I was sure that the outcome would be devastating, given my intense feelings of unease. We went home to collect ourselves and try to relax. After the

MRI, I entered Roberto's ward, and the air was thick with aggression; accusations hung like daggers from the very fibre of the building. A telltale bottle of "special" water on the night stand, and a packet with an assortment of food and olive oil was on the tray, making my entire being shake uncontrollably. Fear gripped my entire being. Roberto was totally exhausted, in excruciating pain, and totally convinced that I had mistreated and disrespected his saintly parents and his brother. They had driven hundreds of kilometres, four hundred kilometres round trip to be exact, to share their displeasure with their son about me not following their instructions and being extremely rude to them. They also complained about me "not allowing" Roberto to speak on the phone to them. Once again, Roberto failed to defend me; he was the one refusing to speak to them! I resisted any temptation to explain myself.

After totally exhausting Roberto, he said they stayed about thirty minutes, they then marched out of the hospital and drove home!

The afternoon passed slowly, with Roberto still refusing to speak—although he had obviously spoken to his DNA providers. Eventually the specialist phoned and said that emergency surgery was required to repair a burst urethra blocked by a huge kidney stone. The relief was palpable. Fear of the unknown can be crippling. At least now we had an explanation. Hasty calls were made, and my family reassured us, their relief palpable across the airwaves.

I gathered all my inner strength and phoned Roberto's DNA providers. Instantly there were more accusations: I was still lying and there was no possibility of an operation. They insisted on speaking to Roberto. Once again, he refused to take the phone, and I was condemned for refusing them access to their off-spring! Once again, I was sure that when this ordeal was over, Roberto would never clarify that he was the one who didn't want to speak to them.

Roberto was wheeled back into his ward after his surgery. He was still groggy from the anaesthesia and was hooked up to several drips and a catheter. The gentle, professional nurse eased himonto the desperately neede bed-pan. He hadn't had any relief since Wednesday morning. We closed the curtain, to give him the privacy he desperately needed.

The bedside phone jangled incessantly—some well meaning cleaner had reconnected it! It would stop for a few seconds and then clang relentlessly into the stillness of Roberto's relief, which was both physical and emotional. It stopped and then screeched again.

I felt behind the curtain and grabbed the phone, whispering, "Hello," unwilling to break the peaceful aura which surrounded the extremely relieved Roberto.

The tirade began immediately:—"Why you speak phone? Where Roberto? Give phone Roberto now!"
Very calmly and quietly, I replied, "Roberto is on the bed-pan and can't speak right now."
The aggression was palpable down the line; the phone exploded in my ear with unabashed hatred. "Give phone Roberto *now!*" Lucifer screamed.

He screamed so loudly that even the nurse looked up, horrified at this unreasonable outburst. A vision of his pinched red face with his thin spiteful lips drawn taut against his teeth crossed my mind, and I could almost feel the spittle spraying from his vile mouth land on my cheek; I even unconsciously wiped my cheek! I slammed the phone down, cursed audibly, and unplugged it. Devastated by this latest round of relentless verbal and emotional abuse, I lay down on the sofa and quietly sobbed, my entire body wracked with frustration and humiliation that filled my being from the tips of my toes to the top of my pounding head. *Oh Lord,* I thought, *what I have ever done to deserve to be treated like this?*

Roberto pretended to be oblivious to my all-consuming distress and quietly drifted off into total oblivion.
My precious girls and I slept the sleep of the dead for the first time since our ordeal started; we awoke to the warmth and support of Abigail and Bruce, bustling about in the kitchen. They proceeded to respectively take up residence in my chaotic kitchen and next to Roberto's bed. Abigail prepared lunches and Bruce served as moral and emotional support for Roberto.

By ten o'clock, I had received four more abusive calls for lying about the operation, not administering the azeite, unplugging the phone, and not being at the hospital. No explanations from me would change their minds. They didn't even listen to anything I had to say. Aradia and Lucifer continued to hurl abuse upon me like there was no tomorrow.

Eventually, we retired, emotionally flattened by the constant barrage of verbal and emotional abuse—and the sheer magnitude of the hatred that had been unleashed on us. To this day, I can't establish if my precious girls and I were more devastated by Roberto's ordeal or by the unbridled venom that was unashamedly inflicted on us.

Monday dawned bright and full of promise. With the ordeal over, Ashley and Ketiwe returned to school. My mom, Alexis, and I made our way to the clinic. Once again, I had an intensely uneasy feeling in the pit of my stomach.

Roberto was all smiles while sitting up, obviously glad to be pain free. We chatted amicably, and all of a sudden, my stomach clenched and a deep feeling of evil filled my entire being. My mouth went completely dry, and the hairs on the back of my neck stood up. I was shocked; the only time I ever got that extreme feeling was when Aradia or Lucifer were in close proximity to me. Alexis glanced at me; her eyes grew wide and her body noticeably stiffened. As I turned to the door, in walked Roberto's DNA providers.

Their faces were pinched, their lips pencil thin, accusing eyes heaping venom on us all. Roberto's calm, relieved aura evaporated like an early morning valley mist. He visibly stiffened and turned white, a forty-seven-year-old man reduced to a quivering wreck! The tension in the ward was palpable. The silence was deafening. Aradia and Lucifer totally ignored us while literally pushing me out of the way to get next to Roberto's bedside. Our attempts at strained greetings were totally ignored. Roberto looked more terrified by the instant.

In that very awkward moment, my phone rang, shattering the silence. It was a potential client I'd been pursuing for months. He had to see me now, as he was on his way back to his head office. There was no question but I had to see him. As we had all come in one car, we would all have to leave. Roberto begged us to stay. My mind weighed up my options: What can really happen? I was sure he'd be safe. After all, it was his DNA providers; maybe they would be kind, perhaps they really did care how Roberto was doing. Another factor was that Roberto was always telling me that I had to keep clients happy.

Safe? How wrong I was!

Aradia and Lucifer had driven hundreds of kilometres to literally shout and scream at their eldest son, who had been critically ill. They berated him because I didn't follow their bizarre instructions and complained to him that I had been extremely rude and uncooperative. They berated him for thirty minutes and then turned and left, not before making him promise to phone Claude and apologise for not calling him when he first became so very ill.

At Roberto's first check-up with the specialist, I casually asked what would have happened if he had been given olive oil when he was admitted to the clinic. The specialist was horrified at the idea and said that his colon could have burst, as the kidney stone was so big it was blocking the urethra and pushing on the bowel, creating a blockage there as well. If I had given Roberto the azeite, his colon could have burst, and I'm sure I would have been accused of another misdemeanour and the DNA providers would deny any knowledge of insisting that I administer the azeite.

Bright and early on Wednesday, Roberto returned home, catheter in place, sensitive and totally emotionally and physically drained. There had been an unease between us since his DNA providers' tirade. I did not want to further distress him while he was still in hospital, and he was desperate to unleash his frustration on me for upsetting Claude, Aradia, and Lucifer.

Within ten minutes of returning home, he picked up the phone and called Claude and Aradia to apologise for my bad behaviour. He believed that I must understand it was just easier this way, otherwise they wouldn't stop. It didn't matter what they said about me, it was just easier. For whom, pray?

In that moment, I truly disliked Roberto with every fibre of my being and vowed that I would never again back down. A black eye would heal but these scars ran deep and clogged my heart with bitter contempt, filling my mouth with a taste far more vile than bile—both lingering long after Roberto's physical encounter was forgotten. The contempt I felt for Roberto for totally accepting how they treated us hardened my heart in a way I cannot explain.

Aradia's evil was certainly turned onto her own blood. Never in my wildest imaginings would I have thought the evil would have been turned onto Roberto. So ultimately she won again. I made a solemn vow to myself to never deal with them again, regardless of Roberto's ranting and raving.

After his illness, there was a silent, swirling unease between Roberto and me. I think in his heart he knew that what happened when he was ill was finally the straw that broke the camel's back. I had finally had enough. I was no longer scared of Roberto or his family.

About a week after he was discharged from hospital, I stood in our kitchen and share my vision with Roberto, about seeing Aradia with the voodoo dolls of me and the girls. He immediately jumped to her defence and insisted she would never do that. In my frustration and pain, I angrily retorted, "I hope whoever sent that curse to us gets it back and they break their arm!"

Roberto just glared at me and shook his head.

A week later, my precious mother bumped into Aradia in Krugersdorp—a very rare occurrence—and lo and behold, her arm was in a sling. The wheel does turn. Roberto had no idea that she had fallen and hurt her arm badly. Aradia had simply not told him.

LUCIFER'S DEATH—JUNE 2010

In June 2010, World Cup fever hit South Africa with a big bang. Roberto, Ketiwe, our home help, and I had great fun blowing our vuvuzelas at noon on the day of the opening ceremony. We were dressed in our World Cup t-shirts and sang the national anthem together with great gusto (if very off tune). We had our own little celebration 200 kilometres away from any action; Alexis, Ashley, and Jan, were at one of the theme parks in Johannesburg in the midst of the main celebrations. We were all in good spirits.

Wednesday, 27 June 2010, was much anticipated as Portugal was playing Spain. Roberto was looking forward to watching the game on TV. When he came home from work, however, he had the telltale deep furrow between his eyes. He wouldn't comment on what had upset him, but I knew with every fibre of my being that it was something to do with his DNA providers.

At eight o'clock, Aradia phoned—a sure sign of trouble. After the normal beating around the bush, Roberto eventually told me that Lucifer had not been feeling well and was now sleeping after Aradia had given him some medication. I was feeling very nervous and had an intense sense of discord deep within my being.

I drove Alexis and Jan crazy, as I phoned them many times to ask how they were. Alexis and Jan were at a resort in Rustenburg with Jan's family for a few days.

At around nine o'clock, Ashley's beloved little Yorkie gave birth to four adorable puppies. The feeling of discord didn't abate—it intensified as the night wore on. At eleven, Aradia phoned Roberto to say there was something very wrong with Lucifer, and she was waiting for the ambulance. She refused to elaborate and cut the conversation short.

By one o'clock, she hadn't phoned back. Roberto tried to raise Claude. His phone was switched off. So he phoned Aradia again. She finally admitted the truth: Lucifer had died before she phoned him the first time; she was waiting for the mortuary to collect his body before she actually told Roberto that his father was dead.

Roberto was strangely quiet. I gave him my condolences and advised the girls to do the same. It was a very strained, quiet time. After Roberto's stint in the clinic, we had had just two brief encounters with Roberto's DNA providers—both very distressing.

Alexis had turned twenty-one in September 2009, and our little family, which included Jan, had gone to a game park for the weekend. Her birthday celebration started with all the waiters and kitchen staff from the resort presenting Alexis with a beautifully decorated cake, which read "Happy Birthday Jan." while doing a traditional welcoming dance around our table and singing African songs of blessing for a beautiful, kind, amazing *makoti* (young lady) who had just come of age. It was very moving to see this totally unsolicited outpouring of love and admiration for my precious gift from God on this, her official coming of age.

The other guests were enthralled, and eventually the entire restaurant sang "Happy Birthday" to Alexis while she stood in the centre of the circling, dancing, ululating staff. My heart was filled to capacity with love and pride. When I asked the head waiter why they had done that, he said they had never come across a kinder, lovelier young lady ever. Confirmation again from complete strangers that Alexis radiated kindness, selflessness, generosity, and love.

Why had they used the name Jan? Our server had asked Jan for Alexis's name. He had misunderstood, thinking she was asking his name! Hence the confusion.

Afterwards, Ketiwe recounted this incident to my precious mother, saying simply, "The whole world loves my sissy Alexis. No one can help just falling in love with her cause her face is very beautiful, but most of the beauty comes from her spirit." Once again, out of the mouths of babes . . .

We then proceeded to drive through the vast game park, eagerly watching the animals and shrieking in fear and delight as we turned a blind corner and almost drove straight into a gigantic bull elephant strolling across the road. We were all enthralled. Ketiwe was so excited and engrossed that her eyes were shining and she simply couldn't sit still.

Eventually, we left the park and made our way home. We arrived home at seven, relaxed and happy after a truly delightful, happy day. Only then did we realise that our cell phones had been in a bag in the boot.

Our phones all had several congratulatory messages for Alexis's birthday; Roberto's cell phone had fifteen missed calls from Lucifer, and Alexis's had ten. A dark shadow passed over Alexis's face as Roberto's entire demeanour changed. Just then Alexis's phone rang once again. When she answered the phone, she was greeted with Lucifer's violent verbal barrage: "Why you no pick you phone. You rude like you mother. You stop you dad pick he phone [you stopped your father from answering his phone]. You make me throw me phone on floor. You happy now, huh huh." He then promptly ended the call.

Alexis was literally shaking, with huge tears streaming down her beautiful face. I was furious. Roberto just stood there, motionless. His eyes were once again pinpricks, with a deep furrow between his eyebrows. As I engulfed Alexis in my arms to consol her, Roberto's phone shrilled.

Roberto was greeted with another barrage of rage. Lucifer berated him for not answering his phone. Roberto tried in vain to explain that the phones had been left in the boot. Lucifer was furious that Roberto was not at his beck and call. Eventually Roberto just stood motionless, with a look of total despair on his sad face, until Lucifer stopped screaming at him. Roberto ended the call by apologising profusely to Lucifer for our bad behaviour.

Once again Roberto's DNA providers had succeeded in spoiling a perfect celebration, ending a lovely day with a huge amount of sadness and discord.

The other time we had contact with Roberto's DNA providers was Christmas Eve of 2009. This was on Roberto's insistence.

He still hankered after acceptance from his DNA providers. He felt that no matter what, they were still his parents. Over our thirty-plus years together, he had only admitted to me twice that their behaviour was despicable and blatantly cruel. He confirmed that none of us deserved to be treated with utter disrespect and be so humiliated by them. But in his heart, he just wanted them to love, accept, and respect him for who he was and the choices he made for his life. In one of these revelations of his true, very well-hidden feelings, he admitted that it hurt him deeply when they depicted me as a rude, uncaring "pades puta." He knew I was kind, generous, and helpful to others; he also knew I had mentored countless people within our community.

Roberto was such a different person when he wasn't in contact with his DNA providers. He was kind and gentle, and we all joked with one another constantly. He helped my precious girls with their school projects, attended school functions, and absolutely loved taking us all for "a quick coffee"—his absolute best treat.

With much trepidation, we arrived at their house at around eight thirty on Christmas Eve of 2009, having driven through from Standerton.

Lucifer didn't greet any of us, he just sat at the dining table, clutching the TV remote, which was locked onto a Portuguese show. Every time one of us spoke, he turned the volume up.

In all her innocence, our little blessing, Ketiwe, asked with great concern, "Shame my mommies, is that man so sad because he doesn't speak English and he is deaf? We need to pray for God to make him happy. He has the angriest face I have ever seen. Why are we at his house when he doesn't want us here?" Out of the mouths of babes!

Aradia had set a side-table with leftovers from the lunch they had enjoyed with Claude, Morrisa, Polly, and Tracy. She didn't even have the courtesy to warm any of the food up. Her phone kept ringing and she answered calls from Claude and then Morrisa and then Claude again.

I managed to catch Roberto alone and asked him why we were there, when they clearly did not want us there. His sad reply was that both Aradia and Lucifer had phoned him and insisted that we spend Christmas Eve together. We ate the leftover lunch and made a hasty departure by ten o'clock.

Lucifer totally ignored us when we left, refusing to move from his spot in front of the blaring television set.
Late that night, Roberto confided in me that Lucifer told him he wanted us to come to dinner so Alexis and I could apologise to him personally for the entire phone saga at her birthday. He also wanted Roberto to apologise to him personally. Roberto was mortified, extremely hurt, and very embarrassed.

After hearing about his father's death, Roberto spent a very restless few hours and then got up at four thirty, bathed, and left for Krugersdorp. He spent the day at Aradia's house and returned by five in the afternoon. The funeral was to take place the following Tuesday.

And with that date set the true venom and hatred this family felt for me and my precious girls; once again, it was to be heaped upon us like burning ashes.

Aradia, Claude, and Marcell paid for a half-page obituary in the Portuguese paper, announcing Lucifer's death. They refused to include Ketiwe's name in the family listing. The reason: "People will think you had an affair with a *prêta!*" Laughable. Like one of us would have an affair and then bring up the child in our own home? Ketiwe was very dark skinned, so it was impossible for her to be the product of a mixed union. My precious girls and I decided to just let their small minds be; as long as people who mattered to us treated Ketiwe as a true member of our family, we wouldn't bother with their cruel discrimination.

We were then informed that we had to produce a loving message that would appear in the pew leaflet at the funeral service. Roberto suggested that we just be listed as part of the family. No, not good enough! We had to write something meaningful. Roberto absolutely could not come up with a single kind word to describe Lucifer. Eventually, on Roberto's insistence, Alexis searched the Internet for funeral messages and forwarded one to Claude. Once again, they refused to include Ketiwe as one of Roberto's daughters.

Tuesday, 29 June 2010, the day before the funeral, dawned bleak and icy. The wind was howling, ripping through everything in its path, with icy barbs freezing everyone to their core. This mimicked Roberto's mood.

At nine o'clock, Roberto instructed me to take our BMW to be washed and polished. The car wash said I could return at eleven to collect the car. Roberto wanted to leave for Johannesburg by one. I returned at elen thirty. The car wasn't finished, they informed me, and asked me to return at noon. I smelt a rat but just left it.

When I returned, I went to inspect the car, although the manager was trying her utmost to distract me. The entire inside of the car was sopping wet. My already frozen heart stopped beating. Someone had opened the driver's window when they parked the car under the wash! They were frantically trying to suck up all the water and dry the car out.

I was petrified to go home. I phoned Alexis to explain the situation and to get moral support for when I had to tell Roberto. He reacted just as I had anticipated: He was furious and blamed me for the car wash mistake. He took it as a personal conspiracy to make us late getting to Krugersdorp. He would not see or listen to reason.

Eventually, Roberto and I collected the car and drove to Krugersdorp. Alexis, Ashley, Ketiwe, and my precious mother all opted to squash into my mother's tiny car rather than drive with Roberto, who was worse than a bear with a sore head.

My instinct was to giggle uncontrollably. It was freezing cold, and water was oozing out of the seats. Roberto refused to sit on a towel, and I could see his very obvious distress on sitting on a wet seat for two hours. He was totally unreasonable and refused to speak to me. He was downright rude. As always, to mask my intense sadness at being treated with such disdain for something that was absolutely no fault of my own,

I became extremely quiet. I immersed myself in my own little world of kindness, love, and understanding. Trust me, a 200-kilometre drive can be excruciating.

As usual, he didn't have the skills to deal with his conflicting emotions. Many months later he confided that he did actually find the entire wet car ordeal, in the circumstances, very funny. He said his instinct was to reveal his innermost thoughts, that Lucifer had made that happen as punishment for not apologising to him! My sentiments exactly. Roberto said at that stage, he just couldn't say anything against his DNA providers and was completely stressed about what was going to happen at the funeral. So true to form, instead of just chatting to me and sorting things out, he spat out the usual "There's fuck all to discuss." I was once again ignored.

Eventually we arrived at Aradia's house; her greeting to us was, "What you wear tomorrow? What the *meninas* [little girls] wear? What you do with prêta [meaning Ketiwe]?"
Roberto looked totally confused. He had no idea what we were wearing, and of course Ketiwe was coming with us. What were we supposed to do with her?

Aradia became very aggressive and insisted that we all wear black from head to toe; she also demanded that we leave Ketiwe somewhere. She was very worried that someone would think Roberto had had an affair! My instinct was to retort, "Just because your husband bonked up a storm with any woman that would have him doesn't mean that Roberto has." But I kept that thought to myself.

Roberto then became very agitated, as none of us had brought anything black to wear. He wanted to rush out and buy new attire for all of us. I flatly refused. None of us, including Roberto, believed that you needed to wear black to a funeral. Wearing black doesn't affirm your sense of loss or show respect for the deceased.
As we were leaving later that evening, I noticed a huge photo of Lucifer on the side board, his thin mean mouth without a hint of a smile. His harsh, tiny eyes glared at the lens. It felt as though his blank stare followed us out the door. An involuntary shudder passed though my being.

In that instant I recalled the spectacle that unfolded in August of 1995 when our dear Papa passed on while quietly holding Alexis hand.

After he passed, Roberto and I went to fetch Kate from a school function. As we pulled up to the house we heard a loud voice coming from behind the high walls of the house. We were quite shocked and approached the gate with caution. The spectacle that greeted us was very sad, but very comical at the same time.

Kate and I stood transfixed as the ethereal sight greeted us: To our right Luke stood on the raised grass landing sobbing uncontrollably. His huge sagging stomach shaking like a mound of freshly set jelly. Tears streamed down his bright red face which mingled with the mucous from his streaming nose and gathered into his wild untrimmed beard. His wife Lavender stood there transfixed dragging deeply on the endless stream of cigarettes that never left her fingers or lips.

Directly across from him, illuminated under the yellow veranda light stood Etha. Her lanky, extra long arms stretched heavenward, her bespectacled face turned towards the light which bathed her in a scary yellow glow. She swayed trance like and shouted "Praise God! Hallelujah! My Father has gone home! Hallelujah. Praise God. Thank you Lord.!"

It was the most disturbing sight I have ever witnessed. This chanting continued unabated until the undertaker reversed out of the drive way. When the under takers brought Papa on the gurney out of the front door in utter shock and disbelief at the spectacle that greeted them, both of the young men stumbled and almost sent Papa's ravaged body flying onto the porch where it would of landed at Ethas feet!

If this hadn't of been so heart wrenching it would of been extremely comical. These young men who worked for the undertakers had removed countless corpses while Papa was with the family as he gently and prayerfully helped them come to terms with the death of their loved one. Now when they removed this dignified, powerful man's corpse they witnessed such a bizarre uncalled for spectacle. You can choose your friends but you can't choose your family. And this bizarre show of supposed grief from people who had seldom attended the hundreds of military functions, church services and award ceremonies that me, my sisters and our children had attended often, without question in, affirmation of the, love and kindness he showed to us and our children.

After the extremely uncomfortable visit with Aradia, with intense relief, we checked into a guest house. After all the tension of the day, we were both exhausted and fell asleep the instant our heads hit the pillows. My precious girls and my mom met us at the guest house the following morning at eleven o'clock, after having spent the night at my mothers home. We were to leave for the church by eleven fifteen.

When we went to leave, Roberto's BMW wouldn't start. Later we were to discover that when the car was flooded, the ignition became wet and full of soap, so it was sticking. My precious girls still insisted on going in the car with their beloved Granny.

At the church, Morrisa made a big show of stomping off when we approached. My precious girls (all three of them), my mom, and I hung back and waited on the sidelines. I lip read a disturbing transfer of barbed words between Roberto and Marcell. Marcell insisted that Roberto come and check the coffin with him, saying, "In this backward country the bodies are *always* swapped and the coffins are *always* filled with bricks!" Lord have mercy! Who in their right mind would want to steal Lucifer's body? A great shudder of revulsion shook my being. For once, Roberto stood his ground and flatly refused to inspect the coffin.

In all the years I have been involved with Roberto's DNA providers, I have come to accept that none of them at anytime will ever see the glass as half full. The glass is always three-quarters empty. If someone wins the twenty million lotto, then it would have been better if they won the thirty million lotto! When Alexis achieved four distinctions in her final school exams, she should have achieved six, and so on and so on. To this day, I shriek at Roberto when he says, "Everything . . . ," or "Always . . . ," or "Everyone . . ." He finds it very difficult to be positive in general, although I have instilled positive thinking in my precious girls and have shown them the benefits thereof. Sadly, Roberto refuses to change his mind-set.

Our little family had not been inside a Catholic church for nearly three years; we had been questioning many aspects of the Catholic religion. We all felt intimidated at the prospect of entering the Catholic church filled with statues and Christ nailed to the cross. As we waited for the people attending the funeral to enter the church, Ashley made a very valid point. In her signature matter-of-fact curiosity and bluntness, she asked, "Mom, why do the Catholics celebrate Easter if they worship Jesus Christ while he is still nailed to the cross? How come in every Catholic church Jesus is still nailed to the cross but then we are supposed to believe that Jesus rose from the dead?" I didn't have answers that would satisfy her curiosity and logic.

The front pew was filled by Aradia, Marcell, Morrisa, Polly (Tracy didn't attend), Roberto, and then two very pushy, rude Portuguese women, who were obviously friends of Aradia. Scorpio and her daughters did not fly over from Australia for the funeral. My precious girls, my mom, and I sat behind them. The entire service was conducted solely in Portuguese, so we were at a total loss and couldn't even ask Roberto what was going on.

Throughout the service, the most disgusting odours, punctuated by audible burps, kept emanating from one of the rude women sitting in front of us. Every now and again, Roberto would glance sideways at her with a bemused look on his face.

At some point, Lucifer's cousin read a letter sent by Natasha. It was six pages long and made no bones about the fact that *she* had been Lucifer's absolutely favourite granddaughter and that he only ever had time for her (regardless of the fact that she had emigrated to Australia more than twelve years previously, while Polly and Kate remained for him to spend a lot of time with). Throughout the reading of this long, tale-filled letter, I watched as Morrisa poked Claude in disgust at the contents of the letter. I wondered if she expected Claude to stop the reading or jump up and say, "Hey, what about *my* children?"

Claude then went on to read a letter from Scorpio, which made quite sure that everyone present knew in no uncertain terms that she was her father's pride and joy and that he only ever had time for her, her husband, and her daughters!

In that instant, as I glanced over at Claude, I recalled the loving, kind, friendly young man he had been before he became involved with Morrisa. He often came to our home just to have a quick cup of coffee or take my precious girls, as well as their cousins, for a spin in his topless volksie, a treat they absolutely loved. We spent lots of time laughing together. He shared our joy when Alexis and Ashley were born. In that instant, my heart was filled with a deep, soul-wrenching sadness at the friendship that had dissipated the instant Morrisa became a fixture in his life. Why was our closeness ended? Because Claude's brother had married a "pades puta" and Morrisa absolutely did not approve of the "pure" Portuguese race being tainted!

When the service over, we filed out of the church. We were last, as everyone had just pushed in front of us. Outside, Rosa pretended that she hadn't seen me. I mentioned this to my mother, who in her innocent, although obvious manner, made sure she caught Rosa's eye and smiled in greeting.

To Rosa's credit, she wasn't blatantly rude to a little old lady. She came over and greeted my mother loudly, kissing her on both cheeks, and then greeted me, filling her very obvious discomfort by informing us that she was a new granny herself.

After the usual commiserations with Roberto's DNA providers, everyone moved off for the cemetery. One of the families that Roberto had grown up with had two daughters of our age. These young women didn't fit into the mould of the perfect Portuguese young girls of the 80s and 90s at all. All of a sudden, I was engulfed in a great big bear hug by the elder sister, her flaming red hair still her crowning glory. Roberto's face melted into a lovely, relaxed smile.

We started chatting amicably; these young women were full of praise for our beautiful daughters and asked hundreds of kind, inquisitive questions about Ketiwe. Eventually, my mom took my precious girls and got into her car. Roberto continued chatting, and by this time, Pedro had joined in the conversation as well. I kept asking Roberto to hurry up, as we had to go to the cemetery.

Eventually, my mother literally shouted out of the car window for Roberto to hurry up, causing everyone to laugh and tease him kindly.

But when we made our way to the BMW, the car wouldn't start! I felt a mild hysteria rising in my gut. In pure desperation, I cried, "God, please, can this car just start, *please*! We are in enough trouble already!" Lo and behold, the car started at that instant.

Alexis drove my mother's car and followed us, but we proceeded to get horribly lost on the way to the cemetery. Roberto tried calling Claude for directions, but his phone was off. Eventually, Roberto's phone shrilled, and it was an irate Claude, wondering where we were; he told his brother how to get to the cemetery, and we soon arrived at the grave side. We were greeted with dagger stares from everyone. Roberto made his way to the grave while my precious girls, my mom, and I stood on the outskirts. After a while, Alexis said I should go and stand next to Roberto, as he was visibly upset. I tried to make my way to stand next to him, but the two very rude women placed their arms rigidly on their hips, blocking my path. I tapped the one on the shoulder and asked quietly if I could pass. The only response I received was a loud, smelly burp followed by a fart! The disgusting odour drifted slowly up past my nose while my eyes smarted.
Seeing my distress and confusion Juan came to my rescue and very obviously moved their stiff arms, thereby letting me pass them and get to Roberto.

After the burial, we made our way back to the church hall for tea. Once there, my precious mother quite innocently went over to Aradia to offer her condolences. Aradia was sitting with Morrisa's mother, the two rude women, and two other younger Portuguese women.

In her kind, gentle manner, my mother started to offer her condolences. Aradia pulled back and began berating my mother, saying, "Where you take my son before grave? You and those *maninas* make my son go late. Why you go drink the tea?"

My mother was horrified. Later, she said as she walked away, she could see it was pointless to try to explain that it had been Roberto, chatting happily with long lost associates, that made us late.

After my mother sat down, another Portuguese woman sat next to her and said, "Why this *preta* here? Why you English here?" While my mom was trying to explain, I walked over and tried to explain that I was the eldest son's wife, Lucifer's daughter-in-law. All she did was repeat over and over again, "No oldest daughter, she live Australia. Why *you* here with these pades and this prêta?" The burping, farting women then came and dragged her off.

I noticed Morrisa go outside. At that time, my mother made her way down the passageway to the toilet. She had shattered her shoulder a while ago after falling down the stairs, and she had been diagnosed with a tumour in her stomach, so my mother was a frail, unsteady, minuscule 32 kilograms. As she slowly walked down the passage, Morrisa barged past her, almost knocking her off her unsteady feet. Morrisa didn't even hesitate. She just carried on, single-mindedly making her way to the snacks table to start packing up the leftovers.

My precious girls and I watched as she packed every last morsel up, with the burping, farting woman helping her. We secretly wondered if she was burping and farting all around the food on purpose, to destroy everyone's appetite. We secretly relished the idea that Morrissa, Claude and Polly would consume left over's which had been enhanced with her burps and farts. Revenge is sweet! I know that when I die I'm on a one way ticket to hell!

In my head I know that these thoughts are really pathetic and ridiculous. The thoughts of a desperate person. However after having been emotionally and verbally abused by these people for so many years I was just desperately clutching at straws, wanting them to suffer just a little. However ridiculous.
I made my way to the toilet, and when I returned, Ashley was visibly distressed; her eyes were wide and her complexion was very pale. While I was in the bathroom, Marcell had cornered her and started shouting at her because she hadn't accepted Cassandra as a friend on Facebook!

Ashley was totally shocked and couldn't believe this spineless move: he had waited for me to be out of earshot before pouncing on my sweet, unsuspecting daughter. My instinct was to confront him, but Roberto asked me not to make a scene. So as usual, I took the path of least resistance and kept quiet.

When we left the church hall, Roberto insisted that we go to Aradia's house. Marcell, Claude, Morrisa, Polly, and Aradia were there. While I sat alone in the lounge, Polly passed the doorway, and I called out, "How are you doing?" Polly was on the verge of answering but then Morrisa forcefully pushed her into the kitchen.

Aradia and Marcell came and sat in the lounge with Roberto and me. The silence was extremely uncomfortable. After a while, Roberto began chatting about soccer and all the excitement of the World Cup. Out of the blue, Marcell commented, "Have you seen Jules Street? It is full of kaffirs and kaffir taxis?"

I nearly choked on my coke. "The 'k' word is not an acceptable term of reference," I said calmly.

"Well, what the fuck is your problem?" he snapped. "Once a kaffir, always a kaffir."

Knowing that any kind of argument would be futile, Roberto and I stood up and left, telling Aradia we were leaving.

We enjoyed a pleasant evening at the guest house with the girls and Jan, and planned to leave for home the next morning by seven.

When we woke, we all decided to first stop and get a delectable cappuccino for our drive home. So instead of making our way to the highway, we drove the opposite way, the cappuccino beckoning.

From the moment we woke up, I had a tight knot in the pit of my stomach. I tried in vain to banish this feeling, praying that we would arrive home safely; I also phoned my home help to confirm that all was well on the home front, to no avail; the feeling intensified!

After parking the car, our little family was merrily walking along past a bookshop when an icy shiver ran down my back. I looked up, and there with his back to us was Marcell. I was not in the mood for our delightful family day to be spoilt, and I knew if we saw him, a confrontation regarding the "k" word would ensue. I stopped dead in my tracks and motioned to Roberto. His response was to turn around instantly; we all did the same and hastily made our escape.

Crisis averted! Roberto had not told Aradia that we would be going for a cappuccino; in fact, we hadn't told my mother either.

We then happily spent time trawling the food hall. The variety of fresh fruit and vegetables was amazing compared to our local branch. I kept feeling very uncomfortable, and at one stage Alexis visibly paled when she was sure she saw Marcell hiding around the corner, taking photos of us with his phone. Roberto irritably told her to stop being dramatic and looking for fault with his extended DNA providers. He said, "Stop making Marcell out to be a total freak; no normal adult would do a thing like that. So just stop!" And so we stopped. I banished the sense of constantly being watched to the depth of my consciousness and had a delightful time with my precious girls and Roberto.

Eventually, at one o'clock, we left for the long drive home.

"All's well that ends well" was my thought as we merrily entered our beloved home in the middle of the afternoon.

THE AFTERMATH

Our little family returned to our daily routine of quite congeniality, minding our own business, happy in our own little world.

More often than not, on Fridays, I prepared chicken patties and we all gathered to construct our own burgers. Ketiwe loved this ritual of making her own burger while often asking endless questions regarding her short life with her brown mommy.

As she constructed her own burger, with an array of delectable fillings at her disposal, she'd ask about her short life with her brown mommy; they had lived in a tin shack, without electricity or running water and often without food. We had always been very honest with Ketiwe about her biological parents. She was a highly intelligent little girl and questioned everything. Aleen and Abigail thoughtfully presented her with a traditional Tswana doll for her sixth birthday. They then explained to her that this would have been the outfit her brown mommy would have worn for special occasions. Ketiwe concluded that since her brown mommy was "grounded" (her term for being buried), she would now be in heaven, wearing her traditional outfit and having tea with my biological father and Papa, while all constantly watching over her.

She knew that her biological father was still alive, although he had AIDS and couldn't look after her. She understood that he was responsible for her HIV status. In her own very determined mind, Ketiwe believed that by following a healthy diet, keeping fit, and trusting in God, she would one day be HIV free. She was also quite sure that one day she would be a famous rock star and we would all live with her in a "Top Billing" home! ("Top Billing" is a magazine show on television showcasing beautiful homes, people, and places.)

We had never told her the brutal truth, that her father simply abandoned her at the hospital while she was gravely ill, never to return or make any enquiries regarding her whereabouts. Roberto and I did see him at court during the foster care hearing. He didn't ask the magistrate for any visitation rights or if Ketiwe was actually okay.

Ketiwe had unshakable faith. At a new church one Sunday, when I was at my lowest and truly ready to just give up, the pastor's wife was praying with Alexis and myself. The next instant another lady asked Ketiwe, "What's your name?"
She responded, "Ketiwe."
The lady asked, "So Ketiwe, what would you like me to pray to God about for you? What do you most need in your life?"
I was sobbing and extremely upset, but I listened with one ear. I was thinking about what our little blessing might say: to cure her HIV, to help her at school, but Ketiwe's firm request was, "Please, ask God to make me a famous rock star and let me live in a Top Billing house with my family!"
I expected the lady to rebuke her and readied myself to protect my precious little blessing.
Lo and behold, this true woman of God didn't question my child or rebuke her. She simply began praying, "Please Father God, will you let Ketiwe become a rock star and live in a Top Billing house with her family?" In that instant, I knew we were at the correct church.
Whenever anyone asked Ketiwe why she was brown but had a peach family (her invented term for white people), she would respond, "My brown mommy went to heaven after she was in a car accident and my brown daddy is like a freezer, so he can't look after me. God gave me to my peach family so that I can be happy and healthy and live a good life."

A freezer, you ask? Near our home, there were two black men who performed as mime artists, doing silly faces and all kinds of bodily contortions in the hopes that people would give them a donation. Ketiwe once asked why they didn't get jobs like her dad or Jan. I explained that if you didn't have an education, it was very difficult to get a well-paying job. I also told her that these men must be respected for thinking out of the box to earn some money with honest work. So she likened her brown daddy to a freezer, as he more than likely didn't earn enough money to support a family.

Should anyone then ask why God sent her to our peach family, she would simply say, "Because I am kind, helpful, loving, generous, beautiful, and honest; I have delightful manners and bring much joy to my peach family!"

Our little blessing makes me smile every day.

On this particular Friday evening, Roberto was late arriving home, and when I called him, his phone went straight to voice mail. I assumed that he was busy with a work phone call. Will I never learn to not assume anything when it is at all possible for Roberto's DNA providers to be involved?

While we all happily constructed our burgers, Roberto pulled into the garage, which is joined onto the kitchen. I could hear him speaking on the phone through his open car window, saying, "I'm really not interested in your and Scorpio's sex life of more than twenty-five years ago!" The kitchen froze! Our curiosity was more than piqued.

Roberto then entered the kitchen, walked straight through, and went out the door into the back garden. He often paced the back garden relentlessly while speaking on the phone to any of his DNA providers. We were left inside, burning with curiosity as to what was going on.

After about an hour, he came back inside, looking shattered and totally exhausted.

Marcell was returning to Australia the following day and felt that it was his "God-given duty"—in his own words—to inform Roberto that he knew that we had gone to the mall the day after the funeral and that should we dare deny it, he had photos and video footage of us! He proudly informed Roberto that he had followed us around the shopping centre for three hours. He had then rushed back to Aradia's house to show her all the incriminating evidence.

My first reaction was, "Is it a crime to go to the mall? Are we forbidden by some unknown law to go anywhere as a family and be happy? Why is it a crime for us to be there but not a crime for Marcell to be there?"

After a while, I also questioned as to why, firstly, Marcell didn't just approach us and greet us and find out why we were in the centre that day. Secondly, why didn't Aradia question Marcell's bizarre and very sick behaviour instead of inspecting all the photos and watching the incriminating video footage and then spend hours on end gossiping about us instead of just phoning Roberto to ask why we were in the centre and hadn't left for home as planned. Isn't that what a normal, loving, respectful, supposed Christian mother would do?

Once again Aradia, Claude, Morrisa, and Marcell proved my point that although they all went to church religiously, said hundreds of rosaries, kissed the feet of Mary's statue (which stands in Aradia's entrance) each time they entered the house, they certainly did not behave as the Bible instructs God-fearing Christians to behave. The Bible is very clear that one should remove the log from one's own eye before pointing out the speck in your brother's eye (Mathew 7:5). I think Roberto's DNA providers skipped those verses in the Bible.

Roberto was completely shattered and very confused. First Marcell had ranted and raved at him for an hour, and then Aradia had gotten on the phone to treat him like a naughty schoolboy for a further thirty minutes.
The long and the short of this complete dressing down included Marcell mentioning that he had not had sex with Scorpio until their wedding night. What this had to do with Roberto almost thirty years later still remains a mystery. Roberto did then manage to get a word in edgewise to remind Marcell that he might have remained chaste and pure with Scorpio but had had many sexual encounters with several girls before his sacred union with Scorpio.

Exasperated that Roberto had brought his sordid past to his attention, Marcell then went on to berate Roberto for the whole hospital incident.

"I know exactly how fucking rude your fucking daughters and your fucking wife were to Aradia and Lucifer while you were in the hospital," he complained. "Aradia, Claude, and Morrisa told me all about that rude fucking woman you are married to."
This floored Roberto, as he always maintained to me that his DNA providers didn't gossip about me. I always said that even if it took fifty years, I'd prove it someday! Well, it took thirty long, frustrating years, but I had proven my suspicions without a shadow of a doubt.

Marcell also maintained that he had paid for Lucifer's funeral, complaining that Roberto, the eldest son, hadn't contributed at all. Later that night Roberto insisted that I transfer R10 000-00 to Claude's bank account. Months later, it emerged that Marcell and Claude had each only give R500-00 towards the funeral. Roberto never established if Claude had passed the R10 000-00 onto Aradia to cover the funeral costs. If Lucifer's funeral had cost anything near R10 000-00, it was truly a rip-off, as there was only one small flower arrangement. The pew leaflet and the coffin were very basic. The snacks were three platters from the local supermarket. The organist didn't charge for her services, and there was only a hearse, no transport for any of the family. There wasn't even a canopy over the grave site.

Throughout Marcell's tirade, he kept saying something about "what happened twenty-five years ago . . ." Roberto was unable to establish what life changing event had taken place twenty-five years ago. I have the memory of an elephant but could not recall anything extra dramatic that had happened then. Give it time. In about two years, it would dawn on me.

Aradia then came on the line and literally shouted at Roberto for daring to go to the mall the day after Lucifer's funeral. When Roberto tried to pry out of her what the huge crime was, she just became more abusive, but without giving a reason as to why our visit to the shopping centre was such a travesty of justice.
After the phone call, Roberto was sullen and furious with the world. We gave him a wide berth, eventually finding solace in our beds. Unable to sleep, Alexis went on Facebook and quite innocently posted the following as her status update:

"What fifty-year-old freak follows people around the mall for three hours taking photos and videos instead of just saying hello?"
My sentiments exactly!

Now, to the world at large, this comment could have been about anyone in the entire universe. Alexis received a few comments: "freak for sure," "maybe pervert is a better term," "WTF," "be careful that this person isn't your new stalker" "doesn't this person have a life," "next time flash them a brown eye—but your brown eye would be so cute. Maybe I should follow you?"

When she read these comments to me, we had a good laugh and totally forgot about it. She had vented in a seemingly innocent manner without actually airing any of our filthy, extremely embarrassing laundry!

Not once did she allude to the fact that she even knew this person; she certainly gave no clue that it actually happened to her or that it was a relative who had done this.

On Sunday, however, all hell broke loose!

Scorpio lifted her tail and sunk her stinger deep into our fragile flesh. Her venom cut off our laboured breath and slowly strangled the life out of myself and my precious girls.

At around midday, Aradia phoned Roberto, irate that Alexis had insulted Marcell on Facebook. No amount of trying to explain that the comment didn't specify Marcell or implicate him in anyway would stop her ranting and raving. The old adage, "If the cap fits, wear it," was shared over and over again, to no avail.

Shortly thereafter, Scorpio started writing humiliating, cruel posts on her Facebook wall for everyone to see, telling the entire world exactly what she thought of us. She seemingly forgot she had left for Australia when Ashley was only a toddler of three and Alexis was a little girl of eight. She knew absolutely nothing about my precious girls, having only seen us twice, briefly, on a visit to South Africa in 2003.

The posts were numerous, reading along these lines: "For the last twenty-five years my brother's wife has irritated me. All her and her selfish brats for daughters have wanted are free food and free renovations. The three of them are selfish. It's me first, me second, and me third. Instead of supporting my poor mother they go shopping. For their whole lives they have only ever thought of themselves. They are always together like there is no one else in the world."

These posts kept coming. Many of her friends commiserated with her, sympathising with her for having such horrible, cruel, self-centred brats for nieces and such a bitch as a sister-in-law. Needless to say, not one of the responses came from anyone who knew us.

We asked Roberto to tell Scorpio to stop airing her filthy linen all over Facebook, but he turned on us and said it was our own fault, becoming very nasty with us.

Not long thereafter, Natasha started her own campaign against us on Facebook: "She thinks her blonde hair and big blue eyes make her innocent—who does she think she is? [Alexis has snow white blonde hair and bright blue eyes.] The three of them are selfish cows. Why are they in this family?"

Then it popped up again! Natasha's post read, verbatim: "Would have thought that would have been the time to help someone who needs it but instead your selfish and hold onto a 25yr old memory which is very much your opinion! Get over yourself."

Scorpio's reply, verbatim: "funny how that 25year old memory comes only now. Didn't seem to pop up during the 25 years of receiving free food and free renovations. Grow up!!! What a pathetic bunch."
We couldn't believe it: For years I had begged Roberto, asking that we not attend the dreaded Friday night meals, and for years I took along contributions that were never touched or rudely dumped in the garbage. I am yet to figure out when we ever received free renovations. When Lucifer did do a few renovations for us, on his and Aradia's insistence, we ended up paying far more than what we would have ever paid a contractor! Then what does Natasha know about this illusive incident that took place twenty-five years ago? She was twenty-three years old. It still remained a mystery. Lastly, they didn't know that Roberto had

taken leave from his job for a week to go and stay with Aradia and help her clean out her dirty, overcrowded, smelly house.

Eventually, after I became absolutely irate and Alexis and Ashley were totally hysterical, Roberto contacted Aradia and insisted that she tell Scorpio to remove all the insults from their Facebook pages. Aradia only agreed after Roberto informed her that I would sue them for defamation of character. Scorpio worked for the police department, and I threatened to tell them that she had been using their state computer to post this abuse, ensuring that she would lose her job.

Through all of this, we didn't stoop to their level and retort in any way. We all, including Roberto, vowed there and then to never have any contact with Scorpio, Marcell, Natasha, and Cassandra ever again.
All spineless Claude could say was, "Alexis shouldn't have said that about Marcell on Facebook."
When Roberto explained that it had been a general comment and only we, our own little family, knew who she was referring to, Claude became like a stuck record, defending Marcell over and over again.
Alexis then blocked Roberto's DNA providers from her Facebook page.

In the October of the same year, Scorpio came to South Africa. To Roberto's credit, he finally showed his loyalty to me and my precious girls and refused to even speak to her on the phone. No amount of begging and pleading from Aradia would change Roberto's mind.

That December, Natasha and Cassandra were in Krugersdorp, and once again their visit passed without any of us having any contact with them whatsoever.

A few months later, inexplicably, Alexis received a notification on her Facebook. It was a conversation Scorpio was having with a woman she had been at school with. Once again, totally unprovoked, Scorpio's venomous nature came to the fore.

Friend: "It's so nice to have found you again. How is your lovely older brother Roberto?"

Scorpio: "Yes it is nice to reconnect. My brother Claude is wonderful and married to a wonderful Portuguese girl, Morrisa. They have two fantastic daughters. Roberto on the other hand married that pades he dated while I was still at school, and we absolutely still can't stand the sight of her, so because of her and her brats for daughters, I don't speak to my brother. Can't understand why he didn't just use the pades bitch for sex like all the other guys!"

Without my knowledge, Alexis then posted on Scorpio's wall: "Can you just leave my mother alone. She has always just kept quiet when you have been so cruel to her. Why do you have to air the filthy laundry on face book for absolutely no reason."

Scorpio: "I'll say whatever I like about your bitch of a mother. Just shut up! Actually just fuck off!" (Oh, so very lady like and Christian! Have I mentioned that Scorpio also claims to be an avid, practising Catholic?)

Friend: "Scorpio, shame, you seem to be upsetting Roberto's daughter. It's better to keep disagreements private? If I remember correctly Roberto's wife was a very quiet girl who always looked like she was in shock!"

Scorpio: "Oh don't worry about them. Everyone knows we all, our whole family, can't stand them. That they are a pathetic bunch and very selfish. Why my brother ever had to marry a fucking *pades* I have no idea."

Alexis: "Scorpio can you just leave us alone. We've never done or said anything horrible to or about you. Please just stop. Why do you have to carry on bullying my mother?"

Scorpio: "Listen here you little brat its way past your bed time. Go to bed and butt out of adult discussions. Or are you going to run to your pathetic mother and complain again?"

Alexis: "Excuse me I am 22 years old. My mother has always just kept quiet and let you all be despicable to her. You have delighted in bullying her for far too long. I won't allow it to carry on. Maybe it's about time for you to actually grow up and just leave my mother alone? Oh I forgot the saying once a bully always a bully!"

Friend: "Maybe it is better if we end this discussion now. Scorpio this young woman seems very upset."

Scorpio then blocked Alexis from her Facebook page.

To this day, we have not had any further contact with Scorpio, Marcell, Natasha, or Cassandra.

THE END—BUT MY BEGINNING!

Since my evil vision in 2009, things had been on a steady decline for me and our family. The list of things that went wrong was almost endless. It felt as though I was covered in a huge black cloud that just wouldn't dissipate. I prayed relentlessly, to no avail. Every time I took two steps forwards, it felt as if I was flung ten steps back.

First there was Roberto's illness. Then after a roller coaster emotional and physical ride, Alexis was diagnosed with Hashimoto's thyroiditis, an autoimmune disease in which the thyroid gland is attacked by a variety of cell and antibody-mediated immune processes. Hashimoto's affects the carrier in several ways. My precious gift from God was affected in every conceivable way: weight gain, depression, mania, sensitivity to heat and cold, fatigue, panic attacks, constipation, boils, memory loss, and hair loss.

This not only devastated Alexis's life and sent her into turmoil but was extremely disruptive and excruciating for our entire family. From being the Head of Learner Affairs who was confident, outgoing, and totally in control of her life, Alexis was reduced to a quivering wreck. It was heart wrenching to watch and exhausting both physically and mentally to get her back to her old self. It took two years for everything to stabilise.

For me, the saddest and most prominent experience in dealing with her Hashimoto's disease was watching her slow emotional decline. As a very private person, I didn't discuss her diagnosis with anyone. By the grace of God, one day I visited my dear friend Niki and broke down, telling her what was going on. She referred me to a child psychologist, a dear friend of hers.

I made an appointment for the Tuesday morning. As if it was yesterday I remember the devastating scene that unfolded that morning. I asked Alexis to take a shower before the appointment. Once again she refused. She hadn't showered in days! Take into consideration that I have never shouted at Alexis in her entire life. Eventually I was standing in Alexis room screaming at her to get into the shower while simultaneously pulling off her sweaty pyjamas and pushing her towards the bathroom and then under the running water. I kept my pose. When she finished I forced her to get dressed. I kept my pose. I then threatened to throw her over my shoulder to get her into the car. Through all of this tears where streaming down her bloated, flushed face. Her swollen body was wracked by her great sobs. I kept my pose. I drove stony faced to the psychologist. I kept my pose. I literally pushed her out of the car. Once I was certain that she was safely with the psychologist I sped off, rounded the corner on two wheels, pulled to the shoulder of the road, slammed on brakes, and then gave into the soul wrenching sobs that wracked my entire being. I sat in my car in the most elite suburb with their trimmed lawns, manicured shrubs, perfectly shaped flowers and howled at God and the universe for allowing this disease to destroy and consume MY Precious Gift from God's very existence.

I am sure I resembled an escapee from solitary confinement of some distant mental institute. After a while through my swollen, sore eyes I noticed a group of shocked gardeners watching me apprehensively, unsure of what to do next. Eventually the bravest of the group sidled over to me with great caution. "*More Mevrou, het Mevrou hulp nodig. Het Mevrou se man haar geklap?*" (Morning Madam. Do you need help? Did your husband hit you?) Oh that it would of been so simple! With a weak smile on my face I responded softly "*Nee dankie meneer my hart is net baie seer. My dogter is siek en ek weet nie wat om te doen nie.*" (No thank you Sir my heart is just sore. My daughter is sick and I don't know what to do)."

This kindly, old African gentleman took his weather worn pitch black hand and gently engulfed my shaking, rough hand in his gigantic paw while he softly said. "*Dus ok Mem, Ons sal vir jou en jou dogter bid. God sal julle al twee better maak.*" (That's ok Madam we will pray for you and your daughter. God will help both of you.) "*Wil Mem water drink?*" (Would you like a drink of water?)

Thinking that this would have a good calming effect I nodded. He opened the car door will shouting an instruction to one of his fellow gardeners in Tswana. A bit confused I followed him out of the car as he lead me gently to an open hosepipe on the pavement. He cupped his grubby hand under the stream of fresh revitalising water, of which I was obliged to drink!

That act of kindness was not what I expected. In our world when offered a drink of water we expect to be served in a glass, however in a parallel world drinking from an open hosepipe is all that is available. When life hands you lemons make lemonade, crossed my mind.

The psychologist referred us to a professor at a local hospital. Alexis was admitted for two weeks, which were life changing. It took two years for Alexis to stabilise and for all her medication to level her emotional and physical being.

Hashimoto's will live in Alexis's body for the rest of her life, but now she is in control of her own destiny.

To this day Roberto has not told any of his DNA providers about the Hashimoto's disease. It is genetic, and I don't carry the gene. Roberto rightly said that Aradia would simply not grasp the magnitude of the effects that Hashimoto's disease can have on a person's life and just say Alexis must get over it. To her, any kind of depression is a sign of great weakness and is to be treated with the attitude of—Pull yourself together. This even though, Aradia's sister, who lived in Portugal and I had never met, hanged herself whilst in a depressed state some years ago.

Besides dealing with Alexis's Hashimoto's disease, my mother had a severe heart attack and landed in ICU for two weeks. She was then diagnosed with a Karsenoid tumour in her stomach, that, by God's grace and a positive attitude, no longer gives her any problems.

During the swine flue outbreak in South Africa, both Alexis and Ashley fell ill with the disease.

The main diamond from my wedding band just fell out. Gone. No trace. There one minute and gone the next, costing R15 000-00 to replace.

On top of all of this, my business went into a steady decline until I stopped operating.
Our van was involved in an accident on the way to an important function, costing us a huge sum.

I was owed tens of thousands of Rands by the provincial government that they simply would not pay me.

On 1 December 2011, Roberto was readmitted to the clinic to repair a hernia and for a prostate examination. By God's grace everything was fine and he was only in the clinic for two days. For obvious reasons, on Roberto's very clear instructions, we did not inform any of his DNA providers.

Through all of this, Aradia was on Roberto's case all the time. All of a sudden she wanted Roberto, Scorpio, and Claude to be joined at the hip after she passed away. She constantly harassed Roberto and insisted that the three of them open a joint bank account so that when she died, the money from the house would all go into one account and then they would handle the account together.

What a joke that would be! Firstly, it's not possible for three people to just open a bank account together, and secondly, really, the three of them having a joint account? How ridiculous would that be?
Eventually I forced Roberto to get a Portuguese-speaking person from the bank to phone her and tell that this was absolutely not possible, unless they formed a corporation, and that would be a problem with Scorpio living in Australia. Oh, but I forgot, they'd lie about that at the bank!

I still can't understand how Aradia and almost all of her associates have lived in this county for almost fifty years and still can't even speak English.

So that door of harassment closed to her, she started insisting that she needed Roberto's passport and identity documents. At this stage Roberto simply put his foot down.

He had been pleading with her, since Lucifer died, to supply us with a copy of her identity document so that she could be included on our funeral policy, so that we weren't saddled with the bills when she passes. In utter spite she refused.

In no uncertain terms, I have made it clear to Roberto that when she passes, I will refuse to pay a red penny towards her funeral.

Both of Lucifer's parents passed years ago, and since Lucifer's passing, Aradia had been like a bulldog hanging onto a bone, trying to pry half the land owned by them from Lucifer's sister. She lived with their parents her entire life, physically worked the land, looked after them when they were dying. She devoted her life to them.

They both passed without leaving a will. Lucifer had been out of Portugal for about forty-five years, only returning three times for brief visits. He didn't deal with their old age, the daily grind of looking after the small farm, the harsh conditions they lived in. But regardless, Aradia wanted that land.

Tongue in cheek, Roberto and I had discussed this many times. Should she manage to steal this land from this simple old woman and then leave it to Roberto, Scorpio, and Claude, Roberto would insist they divide the property into thirds and inherit the middle piece. We would then donate it to build a home for people infected or affected with HIV!

Roberto begged Aradia to just leave it. He wanted no part in taking land he had no claim to from an old woman. Let her leave it to the support system she has had all these years. What would he do with a small piece of land in rural Portugal?

Aradia was relentless. At one stage, she harassed Roberto daily about going to Portugal with her to fight Lucifer's sister. Roberto simply said he couldn't get leave. All of this caused him tremendous stress. This stress was transferred to our home, with Roberto being unreasonable and moody.

From June until December 2011, three confirmed sales of my business fell through for no explainable reason. My frustration levels were extremely high.

On 24 December 2011, I was admitted to hospital for emergency surgery to remove a huge chunk of my forearm. The tissue had died due to a suspected spider bite. I then developed two more spider bites, one on my calf and one on my derriere, in early February 2012. I was readmitted, where it was discovered that I had a growth in my bile duct, which was subsequently removed. I had four anaesthetics all in one week.

By May 2012, I was at the end of my tether. I was physically and emotionally shattered. My faith in God had taken a lot of strain. My mother was the only one still keeping a glimmer of faith alive for me.

Very tentatively, Alexis approached me with the idea of seeing a psychic. For years, I was sure that Aradia had put a curse on me. Initially, I was totally opposed to seeing a psychic; in my opinion, it was unbiblical. Then one day, Alexis saw an advert for a world renowned psychic who did readings over the phone.

Alexis decided to phone and just find out how it worked. Alexis made the call and left a voice mail.

After a while, the psychic phoned Alexis back.

As she listened, she went first snow white, then bright red, then her eyes filled with tears, then snow white again.

Alexis: "I would like to find out how your telephonic readings work please."

Psychic: "You don't need a reading. It's your mother. There is a very strong curse on your mother that has been there for more than twenty-five years."

Alexis: "I don't understand."

Psychic: "You are the only reason your mother carries on living. Your mother is under tremendous stress. Your mother was a young, happy, trusting woman but the curse has taken all of that. Your mother's true spirit has been taken from her."

Alexis: "Why do you say that?"

Psychic: "Everything is going wrong in your mother's life; she is ready to give up. The curse wanted to destroy her. They wanted her out of their lives."

Alexis: "Can you remove the curse?"

Psychic: "Yes; your mother must phone me for a reading. This curse is very strong."

We were totally shocked. With Roberto's knowledge and blessing, I booked a reading for that Saturday morning.

After I phoned the psychic, I learned that more than twenty-five years earlier, a curse had been placed on me by two women who were closely related to Roberto. There it was again: the "twenty-five-year" reference. It hit me like a ton of bricks. Twenty-five years before 2010, when it was first referred to by Scorpio, Natasha, and Marcell, that would have been 1985, the year we were married. What kind of sick, despicable people put a debilitating curse on an innocent young woman just before her marriage to their son and brother? The psychic kept saying the older woman had a deeply lined face; Aradia has very deep wrinkles on her face.

Then a bombshell was dropped: The curse had been renewed three years ago!

In my soul, I had known this all along. It was still devastating to have confirmation that supposed devout practicing Catholics, who had statues of Mary in their home, a rosary in their car, and Holy Water all over the house, would actually be involved in this extreme evil.

The psychic said it was very common amongst the Portuguese community to put curses on people. She said she removed many such curses. She also confirmed that Roberto was scared of Aradia and found it almost impossible to stand up to her. She also said she enjoyed dominating him and forcing him to chose between her and me!

I asked the psychic to remove the curse and then asked her if she would send the curse back to where it came from. She said she only removed curses, she wasn't evil herself. She never placed curses on people; that was of the devil, and she was a God-fearing, honest person.

She said I could expect to have a few symptoms of the curse being removed: I might have an untimely menstrual cycle, an excruciating headache, or a spell of vomiting. Right, I thought, how ridiculous is this now. A bit far-fetched, I thought. The psychic said it was a very powerful curse when it had been renewed three years previously, and the removal of it would be very intense. My bemused thoughts put the psychic down to a dramatist as well!

The psychic started the curse removal on a Sunday. On Wednesday, I started with the most intense, untimely menstrual cycle I have ever had. Coincidence, I thought. On Friday night, something extraordinary happened while I was sleeping.

I was conscious of Roberto in the bed next to me. A very strong force held me pinned to the bed. My entire being was vibrating. I tried to scream. No sound passed my lips. I tried to move. My body was rigid, and an intense, vibrating sense engulfed my entire being. I grabbed Roberto's hand and held onto it with all my might. I forced myself to relax into these feelings and knew deep within my soul that the curse was leaving my body. I consciously decided to just give in to the feelings and begged God to take the curse off of me once and for all, to give me back my spirit that had been so cruelly taken from me out of pure spitefulness.

After what seemed like an age, my entire body made one final worm-like motion. Starting at my head, moving down my torso, through my legs, and eventually with a kick of my feet, I totally relaxed and fell into a dreamless, peaceful sleep.

After a few hours, I woke up. Roberto was awake and said, "The curse left your body earlier. You almost crushed my hand. You were making strange sounds. You made the strangest, worm-like movement with your entire body from your head to your toes. You let out a huge sigh, smiled, relaxed, and slept very peacefully. I hope this is over now."

The next day, I had the most excruciating headache and vomited for hours. I was exhausted. By nightfall, I fell into a deep sleep, waking only at noon the next day. I felt like a new person.

After a few months, I could feel my young self slowly but surely resurfacing. It was like a twenty-seven-year-old veil had been lifted from my being. My precious daughters commented all the time that I seemed like a new person. My goofy, happy-go-lucky, fun nature was visible more and more. I had my power back. I had my spirit back. I was my own person.

Aradia knew that something had changed. She stopped pestering Roberto relentlessly, and if she is still trying to steal the property from

Lucifer's sister in Portugal, she stopped discussing it with Roberto. For the first time in a long time, she recently phoned Roberto and asked how I was. He admitted that he was delighted to tell her that I was happy and healthy and enjoying our life with my three precious girls. He quietly added, "It seems as though the evil that was hanging onto my wife has left."

Aradia hastily changed the subject and hung up very quickly.

I have my faith back. Never again will I allow anyone to be so cruel to me or my precious girls. I will go forward to love life, feel free, and be happy every day.

Have I forgiven Roberto's DNA providers for stealing thirty years of my life?

I let them steal those years from me. I was so very insecure as a young woman that I was convinced that if I didn't marry Roberto, no one else would ever marry me. In retrospect, that is absolutely ridiculous; I am embarrassed to admit that I actually truly believed that. I just didn't know better. I had no one to discuss my deepest fears and confusion with. I have made it my life's work to ensure that my three girls know their true worth and that they know they can speak to me about anything at anytime, anywhere.

No, at this stage, I have not forgiven Roberto's DNA providers, but as I have learnt time and time again, never say never.

I never thought I would have my power back.

But I do!

By the Grace of God I go!